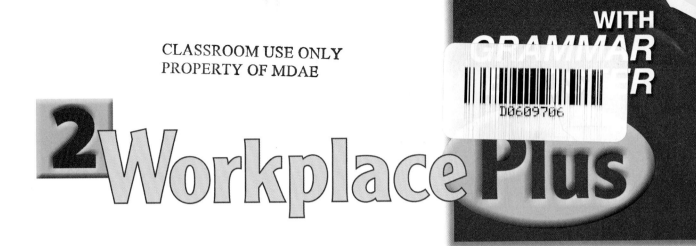

WITH GRAMMAR BOOSTER

2 Workplace Plus

Living and Working in English

Joan Saslow

Regional Consultant Board

Ann Belletire *Illinois*	Sandra Bergman *New York*	Sherie Burnette *Texas*	Michael Feher *Massachusetts*
Susan B. Kanter *Texas*	Brigitte Marshall *California*	Monica Oliva *Florida*	Mary E. O'Neill *Virginia*
	Grace Tanaka *California*	Marcia L. Taylor *Indiana*	

Tim Collins
Contributing Writer

Edwina Hoffman
Series Advisor

Longman

Workplace Plus with Grammar Booster 2: Living and Working in English

Pearson Education, 10 Bank Street, White Plains, NY 10606

Vice president, director of publishing: Allen Ascher
Senior acquisitions editor: Marian Wassner
Senior development editors: Jessica Miller-Smith and Marcia Schonzeit
Development editor: Peter Benson
Assistant editor: Patricia Lattanzio
Vice president, director of design and production: Rhea Banker
Executive managing editor: Linda Moser
Senior production editor: Christine Lauricella
Production supervisor: Liza Pleva
Director of manufacturing: Patrice Fraccio
Manufacturing supervisor: Dave Dickey
Cover design: Ann France
Text design: Ann France
Text composition and art direction: Word and Image Design Studio Inc.
Illustrations: Craig Attebery, pp. 32, 33, 35, 55, 56, 80, 91; Crowleart Group, pp. 14, 15, 21, 33, 39, 50, 51, 52, 69, 91, 97, 99; Brian Hughes, pp. 18, 33, 42, 44, 45, 66, 92, 95, 100, 105; Paul McCusker, p. 23; Suzanne Mogensen, pp. 7, 10, 11, 22, 31, 33, 43, 46, 47, 58, 59, 67-71, 75, 84, 93, 94, 106, 107, 115, 118, 119; Dave McKay, pp. 6; Dusan Petricic, pp. 47, 107; Stephen Quinlan, p. 11; NSV Productions, pp. 5, 19, 38, 43, 47, 74, 91, 95, 98, 102; Meryl Treatner, pp. 6, 7, 12, 34-36, 60, 72, 90, 91, 95, 96, 108, 114, 120; Word & Image Design, pp. 8, 11, 15, 16, 20, 21, 26-28, 39, 40, 43-45, 51, 56, 57, 59, 62-64, 69, 74, 75, 83, 86, 87, 88, 99, 103, 105, 110-112, 114, 122-124, 139-148; Anna Veltfort, pp. 9, 17, 21, 29, 41, 45, 53, 57, 65, 81, 89, 101, 113, 117, 125
Photography: Gilbert Duclos, pp. 2-5, 7-10, 13, 15, 19-21, 25-27, 31-33, 35, 37-39, 43-45, 49-51, 55-57, 59, 61, 62, 67-69, 71, 73, 74, 79, 80, 81, 83, 85-87, 92, 93, 97, 98, 103-105, 109, 111
Grammar Booster: Brian Hughes, pp. GB-12, GB-26; Suzanne Mogensen, pp. GB-9, GB-19, GB-30; Meryl Treatner, pp. GB-24, GB-26.

Library of Congress Cataloging-in-Publication Data

ISBN 0-13-192800-7

2 3 4 5 6 7 8 9 10—WC—08 07 06

Contents

Correlations[1]

Unit	Correlations to National Standards			Correlations to State Standards	
	SCANS Competencies	CASAS Life Skill Competencies	EFF Content Standards	Florida	Texas
1 **Your life and work** page 6	• Understands social systems • Interprets and communicates information • Demonstrates interpersonal skills	0.1.1, 0.1.2, 0.1.3, 0.1.4, 1.1.5, 2.1.7, 2.1.8, 2.3.3, 4.6.2, 7.5.7	A full range of EFF Content Standards is included in this unit. The following are emphasized: • Read with Understanding 1–5 • Convey Ideas in Writing 1–3 • Speak So Others Can Understand 1–3 • Listen Actively 1–4	Student's Book: 35.01, 35.02, 35.03, 35.04, 37.01, 37.02, 37.03, 37.04, 40.01, 40.02, 40.04, 47.01, 47.02, 49.09, 50.01, 50.02 Workbook: 40.01, 40.02, 47.01, 47.02, 49.09, 50.01, 50.02	Student's Book: 35.01, 35.02, 35.03, 35.04, 37.01, 37.02, 37.03, 37.04, 40.01, 40.02, 40.04, 47.01, 47.02, 49.09, 50.01, 50.02 Workbook: 40.01, 40.02, 47.01, 47.02, 49.09, 50.01, 50.02
2 **Your environment** page 18	• Interprets and communicates information • Understands social systems • Serves clients and customers • Negotiates	0.1.1, 1.1.2, 1.1.3, 1.1.4, 0.2.1, 1.4.1, 1.4.2, 7.5.7	A full range of EFF Content Standards is included in this unit. The following are emphasized: • Read with Understanding 1–5 • Convey Ideas in Writing 1–3 • Listen Actively 1–4 • Take Responsibility for Learning 1, 3, 6 • Use Information and Communications Technology 1–3	Student's Book: 41.06, 43.02, 45.07, 46.01, 48.03, 49.09, 49.14, 50.01 Workbook: 43.02, 45.07, 46.01, 48.03, 49.09, 50.01	Student's Book: 41.06, 43.02, 45.07, 46.01, 48.03, 49.09, 49.14, 50.01 Workbook: 43.02, 45.07, 46.01, 48.03, 49.09, 50.01
3 **Your equipment and machines** page 30	• Acquires and evaluates information • Interprets and communicates information • Serves clients / customers • Maintains and troubleshoots equipment	0.1.1, 0.1.2, 0.1.3, 0.1.4, 1.5.3, 1.9.6, 1.9.7, 7.5.7	A full range of EFF Content Standards is included in this unit. The following are emphasized: • Read with Understanding 1–5 • Convey Ideas in Writing 1–3 • Speak So Others Can Understand 1–3 • Listen Actively 1–4 • Take Responsibility for Learning 1, 3, 6 • Use Information and Communications Technology 1–3	Student's Book: 38.01, 43.05, 43.06, 45.07, 46.01, 49.09, 50.01 Workbook: 38.01, 49.09, 50.01	Student's Book: 38.01, 43.05, 43.06, 45.07, 46.01, 49.09, 50.01 Workbook: 38.01, 49.09, 50.01
4 **Your customers** page 42	• Acquires and evaluates information • Negotiates • Understands systems	0.1.1, 0.1.2, 0.1.3, 0.1.4, 1.2.1, 1.2.2, 1.3.5, 1.6.3, 4.8.3, 4.8.4, 6.4.1, 7.2.3, 7.5.7	A full range of EFF Content Standards is included in this unit. The following are emphasized: • Read with Understanding 1–5 • Listen Actively 1–4 • Use Math to Solve Problems and Communicate 1, 3, 5 • Use Information and Communications Technology 1–3	Student's Book: 41.02, 41.04, 42.02, 45.01, 45.02, 45.05, 45.06, 49.03, 49.05, 50.04 Workbook: 41.02, 42.02, 45.01, 45.02, 45.05, 45.06, 49.03, 49.05, 50.04	Student's Book: 41.02, 41.04, 42.02, 45.01, 45.02, 45.05, 45.06, 49.03, 49.05, 50.04 Workbook: 41.02, 42.02, 45.01, 45.02, 45.05, 45.06, 49.03, 49.05, 50.04
5 **Your time** page 54	• Serves customers • Understands systems • Acquires and evaluates information • Interprets and communicates information	0.1.1, 0.1.2, 0.1.3, 0.1.4, 2.1.7, 2.1.8, 2.2.2, 2.2.3, 2.2.4, 2.2.5, 2.3.1, 4.6.2, 6.6.6, 7.5.7	A full range of EFF Content Standards is included in this unit. The following are emphasized: • Read with Understanding 1–5 • Convey Ideas in Writing 1–3 • Speak So Others Can Understand 1–3 • Listen Actively 1–4 • Take Responsibility for Learning 1, 3, 6	Student's Book: 36.01, 36.02, 36.03, 43.03, 43.04, 49.09, 49.12, 50.02, 50.04, 50.05 Workbook: 36.02, 43.03, 43.04, 49.09, 50.02, 50.05	Student's Book: 36.01, 36.02, 36.03, 43.03, 43.04, 49.09, 49.12, 50.02, 50.04, 50.05 Workbook: 36.02, 43.03, 43.04, 49.09, 50.02, 50.05

[1]Correlations are also available at **www.longman.com/correlations**.

Unit	Correlations to National Standards			Correlations to State Standards	
	SCANS Competencies	CASAS Life Skill Competencies	EFF Content Standards	Florida	Texas
6 **Your supplies and resources** page 66	• Acquires and stores materials efficiently • Communicates information • Understands organizational systems	0.1.1, 0.1.2, 0.1.3, 0.1.4, 1.1.4, 1.1.7, 4.5.1, 4.7.2, 6.1.3, 7.5.7, 8.2.3	A full range of EFF Content Standards is included in this unit. The following are emphasized: • Read with Understanding 1–5 • Convey Ideas in Writing 1–3 • Use Math to Solve Problems and Communicate 1–3 • Cooperate with Others 1, 2, 4 • Take Responsibility for Learning 1, 3, 6 • Use Information and Communications Technology 1–3	Student's Book: 35.01, 35.02, 36.01, 36.03, 36.04, 36.05, 37.04, 38.01, 49.09, 50.02 Workbook: 38.01, 49.09, 50.02	Student's Book: 35.01, 35.02, 36.01, 36.03, 36.04, 36.05, 37.04, 38.01, 49.09, 50.02 Workbook: 38.01, 49.09, 50.02
7 **Your relation-ships** page 78	• Acquires and evaluates information • Interprets and communicates information • Understands organizational systems	0.1.1, 0.1.2, 0.1.3, 0.1.4, 0.2.4, 4.2.4, 4.5.1, 7.5.7, 8.2.3, 8.2.4	A full range of EFF Content Standards is included in this unit. The following are emphasized: • Read with Understanding 1–5 • Convey Ideas in Writing 1–3 • Speak So Others Can Understand 1–3 • Listen Actively 1–4 • Take Responsibility for Learning 1, 3, 6 • Use Information and Communications Technology 1–3	Student's Book: 35.06, 36.01, 36.02, 36.03, 36.05, 37.04, 39.01, 39.02, 39.03, 39.04, 41.03, 49.03, 49.07, 50.02, 50.04 Workbook: 36.02, 36.03, 36.05, 39.02, 39.03, 39.04, 50.02	Student's Book: 35.06, 36.01, 36.02, 36.03, 36.05, 37.04, 39.01, 39.02, 39.03, 39.04, 41.03, 49.03, 49.07, 50.02, 50.04 Workbook: 36.02, 36.03, 36.05, 39.02, 39.03, 39.04, 50.02
8 **Your health and safety** page 90	• Teaches others new skills • Acquires and evaluates information • Interprets and communicates information	0.1.1, 0.1.2, 0.1.3, 0.1.4, 1.4.8, 2.1.2, 3.4.2, 4.3.1, 4.3.3, 4.6.2, 7.3.1, 7.3.2, 7.5.7	A full range of EFF Content Standards is included in this unit. The following are emphasized: • Read with Understanding 1–5 • Convey Ideas in Writing 1–3 • Speak So Others Can Understand 1–3 • Listen Actively 1–4 • Use Information and Communications Technology 1–3	Student's Book: 35.05, 36.03, 39.01, 40.03, 42.01, 44.01, 44.02, 45.08, 49.12, 50.02, 50.04 Workbook: 36.03, 36.05, 44.01, 44.02, 45.08, 50.02	Student's Book: 35.05, 36.03, 39.01, 40.03, 42.01, 44.01, 44.02, 49.12, 50.02, 50.04 Workbook: 36.03, 36.05, 44.01, 44.02, 50.02
9 **Your money** page 102	• Understands systems • Acquires and evaluates information	0.1.1, 0.1.2, 0.1.3, 0.1.4, 0.2.1, 1.1.6, 1.3.1, 1.5.3, 1.8.3, 4.5.1, 4.8.3, 6.0.1, 6.0.2, 6.0.3, 6.0.4, 6.1.1, 6.1.2, 7.2.3, 7.5.7	A full range of EFF Content Standards is included in this unit. The following are emphasized: • Read with Understanding 1–5 • Listen Actively 1–4 • Use Math to Solve Problems and Communicate 1–3, 5	Student's Book: 36.01, 39.01, 42.03, 42.04, 42.05, 49.03, 49.05, 50.04 Workbook: 42.03, 42.04, 42.05, 49.03, 49.05, 49.09, 50.04	Student's Book: 36.01, 39.01, 42.03, 42.04, 42.05, 49.03, 49.05, 50.04 Workbook: 42.03, 42.04, 42.05, 49.03, 49.05, 49.09, 50.04
10 **Your career** page 114	• Acquires and evaluates information • Understands organizational systems • Interprets and communicates information	0.1.1, 0.1.2, 0.1.3, 0.1.4, 0.2.4, 2.1.7, 2.1.8, 3.2.3, 3.2.4, 4.2.1, 7.5.7	A full range of EFF Content Standards is included in this unit. The following are emphasized: • Read with Understanding 1–5 • Convey Ideas in Writing 1–3 • Speak So Others Can Understand 1–3 • Listen Actively 1–4 • Take Responsibility for Learning 1, 3, 6 • Use Information and Communications Technology 1–3	Student's Book: 35.02, 35.07, 36.01, 36.05, 36.06, 37.01, 39.01, 41.05, 50.02 Workbook: 35.02, 35.06, 35.07, 36.01, 36.05, 37.01, 39.01, 50.02	Student's Book: 35.02, 35.07, 36.01, 36.05, 36.06, 37.01, 39.01, 41.05, 50.02 Workbook: 35.02, 35.06, 35.07, 36.01, 36.05, 37.01, 37.05 (skills for test taking), 39.01, 50.02

Scope and sequence

Unit	Workplace Skills	Lifeskills	Grammar	Grammar Booster
1 **Your life and work** page 6 Grammar Booster page GB-1	• Takes telephone messages • Leaves telephone messages	• Uses the telephone to make and receive calls • Reads a weather map • Interprets information about weather conditions	• <u>Will</u> and <u>won't</u> for the future • Object pronouns <u>me</u>, <u>you</u>, <u>him</u>, <u>her</u>, <u>us</u> • <u>Would like to</u> + verb	• <u>Will</u> and <u>won't</u> for the future: statements • <u>Will</u> in yes/no questions and answers • <u>Will</u> in information questions • Object pronouns <u>me</u>, <u>you</u>, <u>him</u>, <u>her</u>, <u>us</u> • <u>Would like to</u> + verb in statements • <u>Would like to</u> + verb in yes/no questions and short answers • <u>Would like to</u> + verb in information questions
2 **Your environment** page 18 Grammar Booster page GB-5	• Answers real estate queries • Asks about real estate needs	• Selects housing by interpreting classified advertisements • Inquires about the neighborhood • Interprets lease and rental agreements • Fills out a rental information form	• Object pronouns <u>it</u> and <u>them</u> • Placement of two object pronouns in a sentence	• Object pronouns <u>it</u> and <u>them</u> • Placement of objects
3 **Your equipment and machines** page 30 Grammar Booster page GB-7	• Reports problems with machines • Interprets operating instructions and warnings • Fills out a repair order • Gives estimates	• Reports problems with vehicles and machines • Asks for an estimate • Interprets information to obtain estimates and repairs • Interprets dashboard warning lights • Schedules a repair	• <u>It</u> and <u>them</u> with two-word verbs • The past continuous and the simple past tense • Review: object pronouns <u>it</u> and <u>them</u> • Review: the simple past tense	• <u>It</u> and <u>them</u> with two-word verbs • The past continuous: statements • The past continuous: yes/no questions and short answers • The past continuous: information questions • The past continuous and the simple past
4 **Your customers** page 42 Grammar Booster page GB-10	• Offers and fills out a rain check • Apologizes and offers to correct a mistake • Checks sales receipts	• Interprets advertisements • Compares prices • Makes a return or exchange • Requests a rain check • Discusses a problem with a purchase	• Comparisons with adjectives: comparatives • <u>One</u> / <u>ones</u> • Questions with <u>Which</u>	• Comparisons with adjectives: comparatives • <u>One</u>/<u>ones</u> and questions with <u>which</u>
5 **Your time** page 54 Grammar Booster page GB-13	• Provides schedule and fare information • Explains lateness • Sells tickets • Writes an e-mail message	• Uses different types of transportation • Interprets transportation schedules and fares • Purchases tickets	• <u>Should</u> • <u>Could</u>	• <u>Should</u>/<u>Shouldn't</u>: statements • <u>Should</u>: yes/no questions and short answers • <u>Should</u>: information questions • <u>Could</u>/<u>couldn't</u>: statements • <u>Could</u>: yes/no questions and answers • <u>Could</u> in information questions

Social Language	Vocabulary	Civics/Culture Concepts	Math Concepts and Practical Math Skills	Critical Thinking Skills
How to • Answer the telephone at work • Take and leave a telephone message • Talk about the weather	• Weather-related terminology • Times of day • Meals	• Introduce co-workers or friends who don't know each other. (W)[1] • Understand and use telephone etiquette.	• Understand and state telephone numbers • Interpret Fahrenheit temperatures on a weather map	• Reasoning (uses logic to draw conclusions from available information)
How to • Ask about renting an apartment or house • Talk about a neighborhood • Ask about paying later	• Types of housing • Rooms • Places in the neighborhood • Household bills	• Signing a lease legally binds a renter to its terms. • Expect to pay a security deposit when signing a lease. • Rent may or may not include utilities. • Some landlords do not allow pets.	• Understand spatial relationships • Compare rents • Calculate a security deposit based on rent • Apply concept of "maximum" in making rental decisions	• Decision-making (specifies constraints, evaluates and chooses the best alternative)
How to • Describe a mechanical problem • Leave a machine or vehicle for repair • Offer to call later	• Vehicles • Parts of cars and trucks • Products for cars	• It's OK to ask for an estimate before having a repair done.	• Understand concept of a cost estimate • Distinguish between a span of time and a point in time	• Problem-solving (recognizes a problem and implements a plan of action)
How to • Respond to a complaint • Clarify • Discuss an overcharge	• Personal care products • Medicines • Common drugstore items	• It's OK to ask for less expensive products. • Speak up about a possible overcharge. • Customers are entitled to return defective purchases. • Be aware of terms and conditions for sales.	• Understand and compare prices • Determine cost of items based on advertising and stated limitations • Understand U.S. units of measurement	• Problem-solving (recognizes that a problem exists, implements a plan of action to resolve it)
How to • Buy a ticket • Ask about bus or train fares and schedules • Ask about lateness	• Transportation and commuting	• Be aware of fare-paying policies on public transportation. • Employees are expected to call if they are going to be late. • Understand schedules and plan ahead when using public transportation.	• Calculate wait time • Based on intervals, calculate departure times • Select departure time in order to arrive before a certain point in time	• Decision-making (evaluates and chooses the best alternative)

[1] Welcome Unit

Social Language	Vocabulary	Civics/Culture Concepts	Math Concepts and Practical Math Skills	Critical Thinking Skills
How to • Ask for and offer a favor • Accept or decline an offer • Express gratitude	• Bedroom and bathroom furniture, fixtures, and supplies	• It's OK to ask co-workers for help. • Offer to help co-workers. • It's important to express gratitude.	• Calculate difference between supplies in stock and supplies needed • Estimate supplies needed in a given situation	• Problem-solving (implements a plan of action to resolve a problem) • Reasoning (uses logic to draw conclusions from available information)
How to • Advise someone not to break the rules • Offer a choice • Ask for time to decide • Offer and accept advice	• Work, family, and community relationships • Relating to others	• Know where smoking is prohibited. • It's essential to know and follow an employer's policies. • Express concern for others' problems. • Employees are often entitled to family or parental leave and emergency childcare.	• Determine amount of leave employees are eligible for	• Decision-making (specifies goals and constraints, evaluates and chooses the best alternative) • Reasoning (determines which conclusions are correct)
How to • Warn someone about danger • Report a dangerous situation • Remind someone to do something	• Safety and danger	• Residents are often legally entitled to smoke detectors. • It's a duty to warn others and report dangerous situations. • Express gratitude for help.	• Estimate how often activities are engaged in within a given period of time • Understand periodicity of time in maintaining fire safety equipment • Follow sequential directions	• Reasoning (determines which conclusions are correct when given facts and conclusions)
How to • Ask for information in a bank • Ask how long something will take • Remember something you forgot to do	• Banking and check-cashing offices	• Expect to pay a fee when using another bank's ATM. • Customers are entitled to ask about terms of bank products and services.	• Understand fees and interest rates • Calculate total deposit amount • Calculate checking account balance	• Reasoning (draws conclusions from available information)
How to • Ask about a benefits plan • Remind someone about an obligation • Express sympathy over loss of a job • Suggest solutions or alternatives	• Health insurance • Employer-paid benefits	• Be aware of company-paid entitlements. • Follow the rules set by your insurance company to ensure maximum healthcare coverage. • Express concern for another's misfortune and offer to help. • It is considered rude to ask about another's income.	• Understand concepts of reimbursement and co-payment • Compare time requirements and benefits of vacation and sick day policies • Calculate net pay by subtracting deductions from gross pay • Correct math error in pay stub	• Decision-making (specifies goals and constraints, generates alternatives) • Problem-solving (devises a plan of action)

Acknowledgments

The author wishes to acknowledge with gratitude the following consultants and reviewers — partners in the development of *Workplace Plus*.

Regional Consultant Board

The following people have participated on an ongoing basis in shaping the content and approach of *Workplace Plus*:

Ann Belletire, Northern Illinois University–Business and Industry Services, Oak Brook, Illinois • **Sandra Bergman**, Instructional Facilitator, Alternative, Adult, and Continuing Education Program, New York City Board of Education • **Sherie Burnette**, Assistant Dean, Workforce Education, Brookhaven College of the Dallas County Community College District, Farmers Branch, Texas • **Michael Feher**, Boston Chinatown Neighborhood Center, Boston, Massachusetts • **Susan B. Kanter**, Instructional Supervisor, Continuing Education and Contract Training, Houston Community College-Southwest, Houston, Texas • **Brigitte Marshall**, Consultant, Albany, California • **Monica Oliva**, Educational Specialist, Miami-Dade County Public Schools, Miami, Florida • **Mary E. O'Neill**, Coordinator of Community Education, ESL, Northern Virginia Community College-Annandale Campus, Annandale, Virginia • **Grace Tanaka**, Professor of ESL, Santa Ana College School of Continuing Education; ESL Facilitator, Centennial Education Center, Santa Ana, California • **Marcia L. Taylor**, Workplace Instructor, Joblink, Ispat-Inland Inc., East Chicago, Indiana

Reviewers

The following people shared their perspectives and made suggestions either by reviewing manuscript or participating in editorial conferences with the author and editors:

Leslie Jo Adams, Santa Ana College–Centennial Education Center, Santa Ana, California • **Sandra Anderson**, El Monte-Rosemead Adult School, El Monte, California • **Marcy Berquist**, San Diego Community College District, San Diego, California • **Ruth Brigham**, A.C.C.E.S.S., Boston, Massachusetts • **Donna Burns**, Mt. San Antonio College, Walnut, California • **Eric Burton**, Downington Area School District, Downington, Pennsylvania • **Michael James Climo**, West Los Angeles College, Culver City, California • **Teresa Costa**, The English Center, Miami, Florida • **Robert Cote**, Miami-Dade County Public Schools, Miami, Florida • **Georgette Davis**, North Orange County Community College District, Orange County, California • **Janet Ennis**, Santa Ana College–Centennial Education Center, Santa Ana, California • **Peggy Fergus**, Northern Illinois University–Business and Industry Services, Oak Brook, Illinois • **Oliva Fernandez**, Hillsborough County Public Schools–Adult & Community Education, Tampa, Florida • **Elizabeth Fitzgerald**, Hialeah Adult & Community Center, Hialeah, Florida • **Marty Furch**, Palomar College, San Diego, California • **Eric Glicker**, North Orange County Community College District, Orange County, California • **Steve Gwynne**, San Diego Community College District, San Diego, California • **Victoria Hathaway**, DePaul University, Chicago, Illinois • **Jeffrey L. Janulis**, Richard J. Daley College, City Colleges of Chicago, Chicago, Illinois • **Mary Karamourtopoulos**, Northern Essex Community College, Haverill, Massachusetts • **Shirley Kelly**, Brookhaven College of the Dallas County Community College District, Farmers Branch, Texas • **Marilou Kessler**, Jewish Vocational Service–Vocational English Program, Chicago, Illinois • **Henry Kim**, North Orange County Community College District, Orange County, California • **Dr. Maria H. Koonce**, Broward County Public Schools, Ft. Lauderdale, Florida • **John Kostovich**, South Texas Community College–Intensive English Program, McAllen, Texas • **Jacques LaCour**, Mt. Diablo Adult Education, Concord, California • **Beatrice Liebman**, Miami Sunset Adult Center, Miami, Florida • **Doris Lorden**, Wright College–Workforce Training Center, Chicago, Illinois • **Mike Lowman**, Coral Gables Adult Education Center, Coral Gables, Florida • **Lois Maharg**, Delaware Technical and Community College • **Vicki Moore**, El Monte-Rosemead Adult School, El Monte, California • **Deborah Nash**, School Board of Palm Beach County Schools, West Palm Beach, Florida • **Cindy Neubrech**, Mt. San Antonio College, Walnut, California • **Patricia Peabody**, Broward County Public Schools, Ft. Lauderdale, Florida • **Joe A. Perez**, Hillsborough County Public Schools, Tampa, Florida • **Diane Pinkley**, Teacher's College, Columbia University, New York, New York • **Kay Powell**, Santa Ana College–Centennial Education Center, Santa Ana, California • **Wendy Rader**, San Diego Community College District, San Diego, California • **Don Robison**, Jewish Vocational Service–Workplace Literacy, Chicago, Illinois • **Richard Sasso**, Triton College, River Grove, Illinois • **Mary Segovia**, El Monte-Rosemead Adult School, El Monte, California • **Laurie Shapero**, Miami-Dade Community College, Miami, Florida • **Sara Shapiro**, El Monte-Rosemead Adult School, El Monte, California • **Samanthia Spence**, Richland College, Dallas, Texas • **JoAnn Stehy**, North Orange County Community College District, Orange County, California • **Margaret Teske**, Mt. San Antonio College, Walnut, California • **Dung Tran**, North Orange County Community College District, Orange County, California • **Claire Valier**, School District of Palm Beach County, West Palm Beach, Florida • **Catherine M. Waterman**, Rancho Santiago Community College, Santa Ana, California • **James Wilson**, Mt. San Antonio College, Walnut, California

To the teacher

Workplace Plus: Living and Working in English is a four-level course in English as a second language which starts at the absolute beginner language level.* The course prepares adults for self-sufficiency in the three principal areas of their lives: the workplace, the community, and the home. *Workplace Plus* integrates the CASAS life skill competencies and SCANS Competencies and Foundation Skills with a complete language syllabus and relevant social language.

Communicative competence in English is of critical importance in achieving self-sufficiency. *Workplace Plus* applies the best of current second language acquisition research to ensure immediate survival, rapidly enabling learners to
- understand spoken and written general and employment-related language
- communicate in their <u>own</u> words
- understand the culture and behavioral expectations of their new environment and workplace.

In order to achieve these goals with efficiency and speed, *Workplace Plus* weaves together three integrated strands: workplace skills, language, and life skills.

Course Length
Workplace Plus is designed to be used in a period of 60 to 90 classroom hours. This period can be shortened or lengthened, based on the needs of the group or the program. The Teacher's Edition gives detailed instructions for tailoring *Workplace Plus* to specific settings, circumstances, and groups.

Components
Student's Book
The *Workplace Plus* Student's Book is a complete four-skills text, integrating listening, speaking, reading, and writing with life skills, math skills, civics concepts, and authentic practice in understanding native speech and real-life documents. The book contains 10 units, each one culminating in a concise review section.

The Correlations Charts on pages iv-v indicate how *Workplace Plus* is correlated to the following national and state standards:
- SCANS competencies
- CASAS Life Skill Competencies
- EFF Content Standards
- Florida State Standards
- Texas State Standards

These correlations can also be downloaded at no cost from www.longman.com/correlations. To assist in lesson planning, the Scope and Sequence chart (on pages vi-ix) clearly spells out the following elements for each unit:
- Workplace Skills and Lifeskills
- Grammar
- Grammar Booster
- Social language
- Vocabulary
- Civics/culture concepts
- Math concepts and practical math skills
- Critical thinking skills

In order to facilitate student-centered instruction, *Workplace Plus* uses a variety of grouping strategies: pairs, groups, and whole class. In numerous activities, learners work with others to create a joint product. Those activities are labeled collaborative activities.

Two special features of *Workplace Plus* are <u>Do it yourself!</u> and <u>Authentic practice</u>.
  Because learners have an immediate need to use their new language outside the class, <u>Do it yourself!</u> provides a daily opportunity for students of diverse abilities to put new language into their own words. This affords them a chance to "try their wings" in the safe and supportive environment of the classroom.
  <u>Authentic practice</u> activities create a "living language laboratory" within the classroom. Learners practice responding to authentic models of spoken and written English with the limited language they know. In this way, students build their confidence and skill in coping with the language of the real world.

---

* *Literacy Plus*, which precedes *Workplace Plus*, serves the combined ESL and literacy needs of the pre-literate beginner.

As a supplement to the Practical grammar section in each *Workplace Plus* unit, the Student's Book includes a comprehensive Grammar Booster at the back of the book. The Grammar Booster provides abundant additional practice for each grammar point taught in the Student's Book units. It also includes grammar charts so that students can review the grammar forms and "Things to remember" before they do an exercise. The Grammar Booster exercises can be done any time after the grammar has been introduced on the Practical grammar pages, either in class or as homework. For your convenience, a separate Answer Key is available.

Audiocassettes and Audio CDs

Because listening comprehension is a fundamental survival and success skill for new speakers of English, *Workplace Plus* includes a comprehensive listening strand in each unit of the Student's Book. In addition to listening comprehension activities, there are numerous other opportunities for learners to practice their listening skills. All exercises that appear on audio CD or audiocassette are marked with a 🎧 symbol. A transcript of each listening comprehension activity is located on its corresponding Teacher's Edition page, for easy reference.

Teacher's Edition

An interleaved Teacher's Edition provides page-by-page teaching suggestions that add value to the Student's Book. In addition to general and day-by-day teaching suggestions, each teacher's page includes optional activities, language and culture notes that will help teachers demystify and explain new language to students, answers to all exercises, and the tapescript of each listening comprehension activity.

Workbook

In addition to the ample opportunities for reading and writing practice contained in the Student's Book, the *Workplace Plus* Workbook contains further reading and writing exercises. The Workbook is valuable for homework or for

in-class activities. An added feature is a test preparation activity for each unit, which readies learners for "bubbling in" and coping with the formats of standardized language tests.

Teacher's Resource Binder

These photocopiable support activities extend the Student's Book, enable busy teachers to customize their instruction, and make the preparation of supplementary teaching aids unnecessary. The Resource Binder features pair-work cards, vocabulary flash cards, and extension activities for daily use. In addition, four-skill achievement tests provide an evaluation tool for all students using *Workplace Plus*.

Do it yourself! Transparencies

A special feature of the *Workplace Plus* series is the full-page Do it yourself! illustration located at the end of each unit. This open-ended activity is designed to elicit from students all the language they know—vocabulary, social language, and grammar. The picture provides a clear visual context for practice and helps students bridge the gap between language practice and authentic language use. The full-page illustrations are available as four-color transparencies to be used with an overhead projector. The Do it yourself! transparencies come in a convenient, resealable envelope, along with a Teacher's Notes booklet containing suggested activities.

Placement Test

A simple-to-administer test places students accurately within the *Workplace Plus* series.

Workplace Plus Companion Website

The *Workplace Plus* companion website (www.longman.com/workplaceplus) provides numerous additional resources for students and teachers. This no-cost, high-benefit feature includes opportunities for further practice of language and content from the *Workplace Plus* Student's Book. For the teacher, there are optional strategies and materials that amplify the *Workplace Plus* Teacher's Edition.

Student's Book unit contents
Each unit in the *Workplace Plus* Student's Book uses an integrated five-step approach.

1. Vocabulary

   Essential vocabulary is presented in a picture dictionary format and followed by exercises.

2. Practical conversations

   Simple, memorable model conversations that are transferable to learners' own lives permit intensive practice of vocabulary and key social language. These are followed by lively pair-work activities.

3. Practical grammar

   Essential grammatical structure practice enables learners to manipulate the vocabulary and practical conversations to express ideas of their own.

4. Authentic practice 1

   A unique, real-world listening and speaking rehearsal, in which learners build their confidence and ability to interact in the world beyond the classroom.

5. Authentic practice 2

   A unique, real-world reading and writing rehearsal, in which learners build their confidence and skill to understand and use authentic documents that they will encounter in their own lives.

Review
Following each unit is a two-page review for learners to check their progress.

About the author and series advisor

Author

Joan Saslow

Joan Saslow has taught English as a second language and English as a foreign language to adults and young adults in the United States and Chile. She taught workplace English at the General Motors auto assembly plant in Tarrytown, NY; and Adult ESL at Westchester Community College and at Marymount College in New York. In addition, Ms. Saslow taught English and French at the Binational Centers of Valparaíso and Viña del Mar, Chile, and the Catholic University of Valparaíso.

Ms. Saslow is the series director of Longman's popular five-level adult series *True Colors, an EFL Course for Real Communication* and of *True Voices*, a five-level video course. She is the author of *English in Context: Reading Comprehension for Science and Technology*, a three-level series for English for special purposes. In addition, Ms. Saslow has been an editor of language teaching materials, a teacher trainer, and a frequent speaker at gatherings of ESL and EFL teachers for over thirty years.

Series advisor

Edwina Hoffman

Edwina Hoffman has taught English for speakers of other languages in South Florida and at the Miccosukee Tribe of Indians, and English as a foreign language in Venezuela. She provided teacher training in a seven-state area for federally funded multi-functional resource centers serving the southeastern part of the United States. Dr. Hoffman taught English composition at Florida International University and graduate ESOL methods at the University of Miami.

Dr. Hoffman is an instructional supervisor with the adult and vocational programs of Miami-Dade County Public Schools in Miami, Florida. She has acted as a consultant, reviewer, and author of adult ESOL materials for over twenty years. A graduate of Middlebury College, Dr. Hoffman's doctoral degree is from Florida International University.

Welcome to *Workplace Plus*

➤ Practical conversations

Conversation 1   Greetings and introductions

🎧 **A.** Listen and read.

1.

2.

3.

4.

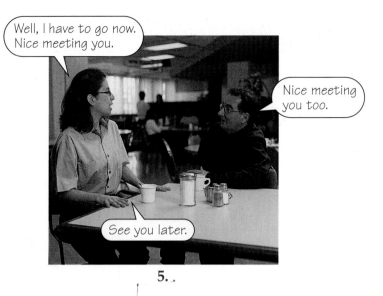

5.

🎧 **B.** Listen again and repeat.

> ➤ Do it yourself!

A. Introduce yourself to a classmate.

B. Now introduce two classmates to each other.

C. Make a chart. Write three classmates' names. Write their occupations. Write the countries they are from.

Name	Occupation	Country
Joseph	machinist	Korea
1.		
2.		
3.		

D. Tell the class about your classmates.

Joseph is a machinist. He's from Korea.

Welcome   3

A. Listen and read.

1.

2.

3.

4.

B. Listen again and repeat.

➤ Do it yourself!

Talk to three classmates. Clarify the spelling of their names.

🎧 **A.** Listen and read.

🎧 **B.** Listen again and repeat.

C. Pair work. **Match each statement to the correct response. Then practice with a partner.**

Statements	Responses
1. Mynumber's9085557806.	a. It's a pickup truck.
2. What's this called in English?	b. Could you please speak louder?
3. What does "breezy" mean?	c. Could you please speak slower?
4. My number is 908-555-7806.	d. It means windy.

Your life and work

Objectives
- take telephone messages
- leave telephone messages
- talk about the weather
- read a weather map

➤ Vocabulary

Picture dictionary

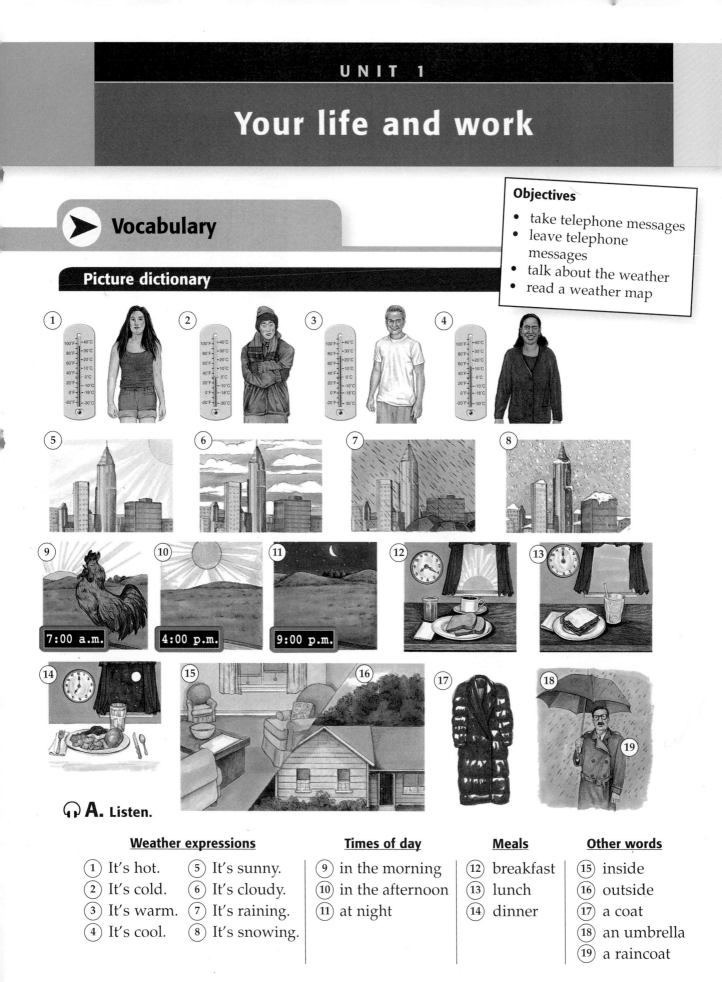

🎧 **A.** Listen.

Weather expressions		Times of day	Meals	Other words
① It's hot.	⑤ It's sunny.	⑨ in the morning	⑫ breakfast	⑮ inside
② It's cold.	⑥ It's cloudy.	⑩ in the afternoon	⑬ lunch	⑯ outside
③ It's warm.	⑦ It's raining.	⑪ at night	⑭ dinner	⑰ a coat
④ It's cool.	⑧ It's snowing.			⑱ an umbrella
				⑲ a raincoat

Good and bad weather

(20) good weather   terrific weather
     beautiful weather   great weather

(21) bad weather   awful weather
     terrible weather   horrible weather

B. Listen again and repeat.

C. Listen to the conversations. Then listen again and match each picture with a conversation. Write the letter on the line.

Conversation 1 _____   a.   b.   c.

Conversation 2 _____

Conversation 3 _____

D. Complete each sentence. Write the word on the line.

1. It's 1:00 p.m. Let's have _____.
   lunch / breakfast

2. It's _____ today. Let's eat outside.
   snowing / warm

3. You don't need your _____ this morning. It's not cold outside.
   umbrella / coat

4. The weather was beautiful yesterday. It was sunny and _____.
   raining / warm

5. We eat _____ in the morning.
   breakfast / dinner

➤ Do it yourself!

> Today it's sunny and warm. I'm wearing a T-shirt.

A. Personalization. Complete the chart about the weather and your clothes.

	Date	Weather	Clothes
Today	May 13	sunny and warm	a T-shirt
Today			
Yesterday			

> Yesterday it was cloudy and cool. I wore a warm jacket.

B. Discussion. Talk about the weather and what you wore.

Practical conversations

A. Listen and read.

A: Copies Plus. Can I help you?
B: Yes, please. This is Jack Santos.
   I'm calling Jim Olcott. Is he in?
A: Yes, he is. Just a moment, please....
   Jim? It's for you.

B. Listen again and repeat.

C. Pair work. Now use these companies and people. Or use your <u>own</u> company and people.

Ace Cleaning Company	Victor Garcia
City Bus Service	Linda Lo

A: _____. Can I help you?
B: Yes, please. This is _____. I'm calling _____. Is _____ in?
A: Yes, _____ is. Just a moment, please.... _____? It's for you.

A. Listen and read.

A: City Rentals.
B: Hello. Is Art Singer there?
A: No, I'm sorry. He's not in right now. Who's calling?
B: This is Ann Chang. When will he be back?
A: I'm not sure. Would you like to leave a message, Ms. Chang?
B: Yes. My number's 555-5021.

B. Listen again and repeat.

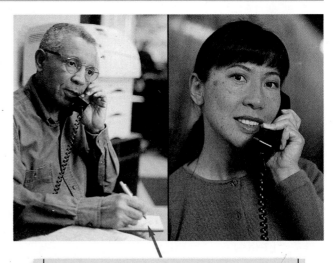

Message *Art:*
Please call Ann Chang.
555-5021

C. Pair work. **Now use these companies and people. Or use your <u>own</u> company and people.**

Clearwater Plumbing	Steven Meng
Blake School Supplies	Tanya Golub

A: _____

B: Hello. Is _____ there?

A: No, I'm sorry. _____ 's not in right now. Who's calling?

B: This is _____. When will _____ be back?

A: _____. Would you like to leave a message, _____?

B: Yes. My number's _____.

Model 3   Talk about the weather. Ask about messages.

A. Listen and read.

    A: Oh, hi, Rita. What's it like outside?

    B: Terrible. It's raining. By the way, are there any messages for me?

    A: Yes. Andrea Lin called.

B. Listen again and repeat.

C. Pair work. **Now use your <u>own</u> words.**

    A: Oh, hi, _____. What's it like outside?

    B: _____. By the way, are there any messages for me?

    A: Yes. _____ called.

➤ Do it yourself!

Pair work. **Create a telephone conversation for the people in the picture.**

Will and won't for the future

When **will** they **be** in? — Later this afternoon.
Where **will** we **eat** lunch on Sunday? — Outside.
Who'll **answer** the phones tomorrow morning? — Ms. Kim.

| will + not = won't | I **won't call** Mr. Kapoor today. I'**ll call** tomorrow. |

A. Where and when will you eat tomorrow? Write the places and the times. Then tell a partner what you'll do.

Tomorrow I'll eat breakfast at home at 7:00.

	Where?	**What time?**
Breakfast		
Lunch		
Dinner		

B. Write short answers about yourself. Use <u>Yes, I will</u> or <u>No, I won't</u>.

1. Will you eat lunch in a restaurant tomorrow? _____

2. Will you eat breakfast in English class on Monday? _____

3. Will you go to China this year? _____

Object pronouns <u>me</u>, <u>you</u>, <u>him</u>, <u>her</u>, <u>us</u>

They called **me** this morning.
Mr. Sorok left a message for **you**.
I'll see **him** tomorrow.
Please give **her** your umbrella.
They ate dinner with **us** yesterday.

Object pronouns

I	me
you	you
he	him
she	her
we	us

C. Complete each sentence with an object pronoun.

1. Do you want a job at Village Paints? Please talk to _____*us*_____ on Monday.
   Marie and me

2. Give _____ an umbrella. It's raining outside.
   Mr. Loyola

3. This coffee is cold. Please bring _____ some hot coffee.

my daughter

4. Please give this message to _____. He's in the office.

your manager

5. Ms. Smith's not in? Can I leave _____ a message?

Ms. Smith

6. Please leave a message for _____. We'll call you back later.

Mr. Black and me

Would like to + verb

> I'd like to leave a message.

> OK, Ms. Perez.

She'd like to		
We'd like to	leave a message.
They'd like to		

I + would like = I'd like

| **Would** | you
he
they | **like to eat** lunch now? | Yes, | we
he
they | **would.** / No, | we
he
they | **wouldn't.** |

When **would** she **like to go**? In the morning.
Where **would** they **like to work**? At Village Paints.

D. **Complete each sentence with a form of would like to and the verb.**

1. I 'd like to leave _____ a message for my son.

leave

2. Please tell Patrick that we _____ to him in the afternoon.

talk

3. Our friends _____ inside. The weather is terrible.

eat

4. _____ you _____ in the morning or at night?

work

5. What kind of a job _____ she _____ ?

have

➤ Do it yourself!

A. **Personalization. What would you like to do tomorrow? Make a list of three things.**

B. **Pair work. Now tell your partner what you'd like to do tomorrow.**

> Tomorrow I'd like to buy a new umbrella.

1. *buy a new umbrella*

2. _____

3. _____

4. _____

Authentic practice 1

With words you know, YOU can talk to this receptionist.

🎧 **A.** Listen and read.

Receptionist: Good morning. Paradise Travel. How may I direct your call?

YOU *This is Jenny Lessing. I'd like to talk to Maggie Thomas.*

Receptionist: Just a minute, Ms. Lessing. I'll see if she's here…. I'm sorry, Ms. Lessing. She stepped away. Would you like me to tell her you called?

YOU *Yes, please. My number's 525-7532.*

Receptionist: 525-7532. And is that L-E-S-S-I-N-G?

YOU *Yes, it is.*

Receptionist: And how long will you be at that number?

YOU *I'm not sure.*

Receptionist: Well, I'll tell her you called.

🎧 **B.** Listen to the receptionist. Read <u>your</u> part out loud.

🎧 **C.** Listen and read. Choose <u>your</u> response. Circle the letter.

1. "Health Care Center. How may I help you?"

   a. Yes, please.   **b.** I'm calling Dr. Flynn.

2. "I'm sorry. She stepped away."

   a. When will she be back?   **b.** Can I talk to her, please?

3. "How long will you be at that number?"

   a. For an hour.   **b.** My number's 223-6511.

🎧 **D.** Listen. Choose <u>your</u> response. Circle the letter.

1. **a.** Thanks.   **b.** Five minutes.

2. **a.** Just a moment. I'll check.   **b.** Yes, please.

3. **a.** This is Peter Miller. Is Susan   **b.** This is Peter Miller. When will she
      Preston there?   be back?

A. Listen to the weather report. Then listen again and check ☑ the weather report you hear.

1. _____ today's weather in Miami

2. _____ tomorrow's weather in Miami

3. _____ yesterday's weather in Miami

4. _____ tomorrow's weather in Los Angeles

B. Critical thinking. Listen to the weather report again. Then answer the questions. Circle the letter.

1. What number did the caller press?   **a.** 2   **b.** 3

2. What will the weather be at night?   **a.** good   **b.** bad

C. In your own words. Answer the questions and then talk with a partner.

1. Where do <u>you</u> get information about the weather? _____

_____

2. Why is it important to have information about the weather? _____

_____

➤ Do it yourself!

A. Write your <u>own</u> response. Then read your conversation out loud with a partner.

Good afternoon. Mark Novak's office.

YOU _____

Oh, I'm sorry. He's not in the office today. Who's calling?

YOU _____

Would you care to leave a message?

YOU _____

B. Personalization. Talk about a telephone call you made.

Authentic practice 2

Reading

A. Look at the weather map. Then complete the sentence. Circle the letter.

The map tells about _____.   **a.** the future   **b.** the past

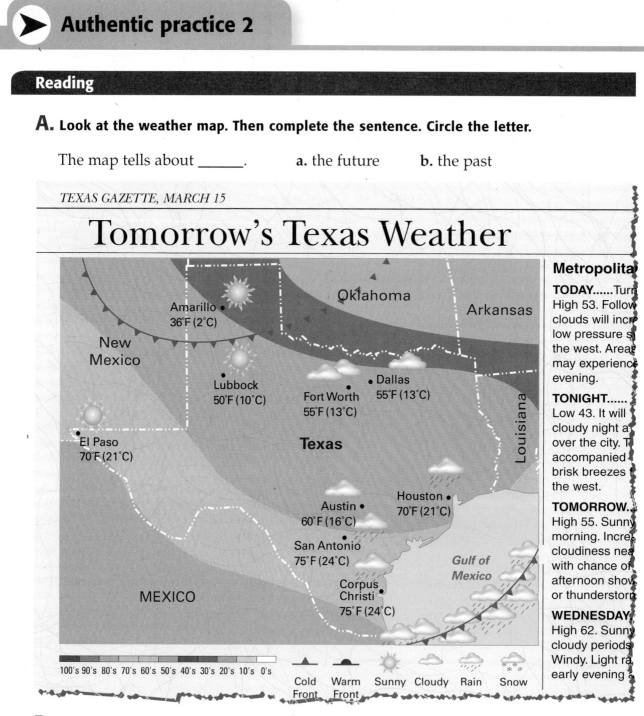

TEXAS GAZETTE, MARCH 15

Tomorrow's Texas Weather

Oklahoma

Arkansas

New Mexico

Amarillo •
36°F (2°C)

•
Lubbock
50°F (10°C)

Dallas
55°F (13°C)

Fort Worth
55°F (13°C)

Louisiana

• El Paso
70°F (21°C)

Texas

Houston •
70°F (21°C)

Austin •
60°F (16°C)

San Antonio
75°F (24°C)

Gulf of
Mexico

MEXICO

Corpus
Christi •
75°F (24°C)

100's 90's 80's 70's 60's 50's 40's 30's 20's 10's 0's

Cold
Front

Warm
Front

Sunny   Cloudy   Rain   Snow

Metropolita

TODAY...... Turn
High 53. Follow
clouds will incr
low pressure s
the west. Area
may experienc
evening.

TONIGHT......
Low 43. It will
cloudy night a
over the city. T
accompanied
brisk breezes f
the west.

TOMORROW...
High 55. Sunny
morning. Incre
cloudiness nea
with chance of
afternoon show
or thunderstorr

WEDNESDAY
High 62. Sunny
cloudy periods
Windy. Light ra
early evening

B. What will the weather be tomorrow? Write one or two words from the box for each city.

cloudy	rainy	sunny	hot	cold	warm	cool

1. Amarillo   *sunny and cold*   4. Fort Worth _____

2. San Antonio _____   5. Houston _____

3. Lubbock _____

14   Unit 1

C. Critical thinking. **Look at the weather map in Exercise A. Choose advice for each person.**

> You're in luck! The weather will be beautiful.

> You'll need a coat.

> You'll need an umbrella and a raincoat.

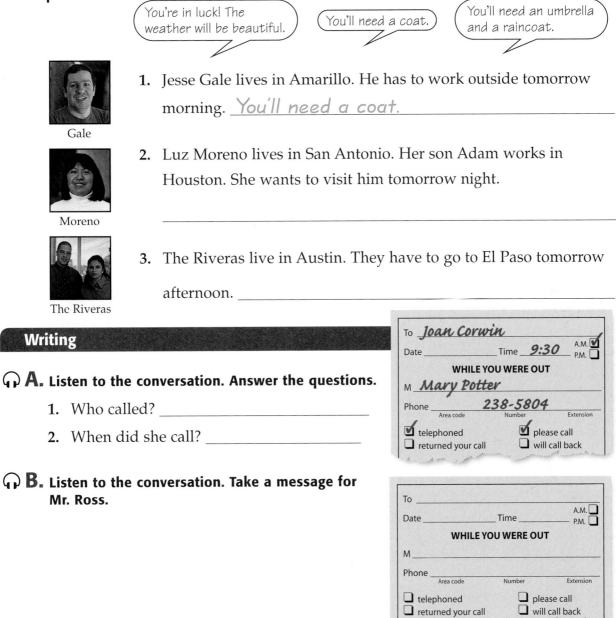

Gale

1. Jesse Gale lives in Amarillo. He has to work outside tomorrow morning. *You'll need a coat.*

Moreno

2. Luz Moreno lives in San Antonio. Her son Adam works in Houston. She wants to visit him tomorrow night.

_____

The Riveras

3. The Riveras live in Austin. They have to go to El Paso tomorrow afternoon. _____

Writing

🎧 **A.** **Listen to the conversation. Answer the questions.**

1. Who called? _____

2. When did she call? _____

🎧 **B.** **Listen to the conversation. Take a message for Mr. Ross.**

To _Joan Corwin_
Date _____ Time _9:30_ A.M. ☑ P.M. ☐
WHILE YOU WERE OUT
M _Mary Potter_
Phone _____ 238-5804 _____
Area code   Number   Extension
☑ telephoned   ☑ please call
☐ returned your call   ☐ will call back

To _____
Date _____ Time _____ A.M. ☐ P.M. ☐
WHILE YOU WERE OUT
M _____
Phone _____
Area code   Number   Extension
☐ telephoned   ☐ please call
☐ returned your call   ☐ will call back

For extra practice, go to page 139.

➤ Do it yourself!   A plan-ahead project

Collaborative activity. Bring a weather map from the newspaper or the Internet to class. Talk about the weather. Prepare a weather report for the class.

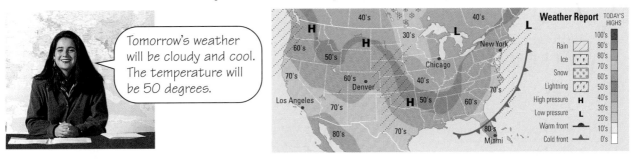

> Tomorrow's weather will be cloudy and cool. The temperature will be 50 degrees.

A. **Vocabulary. Complete each sentence. Write the words on the line.**

1. The weather's _____ today. Take a raincoat and an umbrella.
   terrible / terrific

2. When it's snowing, it's _____ outside.
   warm / cold

3. When it's cold outside, it's a good idea to wear a warm _____.
   umbrella / coat

B. **Conversation. Choose your response. Circle the letter.**

1. "Would you care to leave a message?"

   a. Who's calling?   **b.** Yes. Please tell her I'll call back.

2. "Will you be at that number later this afternoon?"

   a. I'm not sure.   **b.** 535-6622.

3. "I'm sorry. She won't be in today."

   a. Will you be there later?   **b.** That's OK. I'll call back.

C. **Grammar. Complete each sentence with an object pronoun.**

1. They left _____us_____ a message to call the factory.
   my husband and me

2. Did they tell _____ who called?
   you and your friend

3. Ron would like _____ to call back later.
   Mrs. Rivas

D. **Grammar. Complete each sentence with a form of would like to and the verb.**

1. Please tell her that we _would like to talk_ to her tomorrow morning.
   talk

2. _____ you _____ on Monday or Tuesday?
   work

3. What time _____ she _____ lunch?
   eat

E. **Writing. Listen to the conversation. Take a message.**

To _____
Date _____ Time _____ A.M. ☐ P.M. ☐
WHILE YOU WERE OUT
M _____
Phone _____
Area code   Number   Extension
☐ telephoned   ☐ please call
☐ returned your call   ☐ will call back

▶ Do it yourself!

1. **Point. Name things in the pictures.**
   A raincoat

2. **Ask questions about the pictures.**
   What's the weather like today?

3. **Create conversations for the people.**
   A: Would you like to leave a message?
   B: No thanks. I'll call back later.

4. **Say more about the pictures. Use your <u>own</u> words. Say as much as you can.**

LATER

PALMER
OFFICE SUPPLIES

Martin Vargas
MANAGER

October 10

The Corpus Christi Courier
October 10, 2004
RAIN HITS TEXAS!
Ft. Worth · Dallas
TEXAS
Corpus Christi

Now I can
❑ take telephone messages.
❑ leave telephone messages.
❑ talk about the weather.
❑ read a weather map.

❑ _____ .

Your environment

Vocabulary

Objectives

- rent a house or an apartment
- talk about rooms
- ask about the neighborhood

Picture dictionary

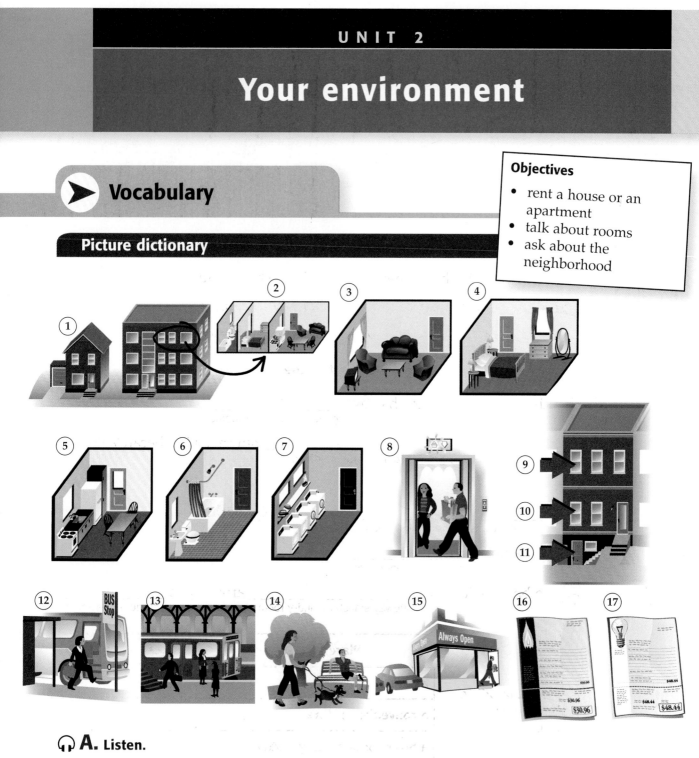

🎧 **A.** Listen.

Housing		The neighborhood	Other words
① a house	⑦ a laundry room	⑫ a bus stop	⑯ a gas bill
② an apartment	⑧ an elevator	⑬ a subway station	⑰ an electric bill
③ a living room	⑨ the second floor	⑭ a park	
④ a bedroom	⑩ the ground floor	⑮ a convenience store	
⑤ a kitchen	⑪ the basement		
⑥ a bathroom			

Expressions of location

18 down the street

19 around the corner

20 across the street

21 next door

B. Listen again and repeat.

C. Where are the people? Listen to the conversations. Then listen again and circle the letter.

Conversation 1	**a.** in the kitchen	**b.** in the bathroom
Conversation 2	**a.** in the bedroom	**b.** in the bathroom
Conversation 3	**a.** in the bedroom	**b.** in the laundry room

D. Complete each sentence. Write the words on the line.

1. The Kermians' new apartment has two _____.
   ground floors / bedrooms

2. The apartment is _____, but that's OK because there's
   on the ground floor / on the fourth floor
   an elevator.

3. There's a _____ in the neighborhood.
   convenience store / bathroom

4. There's a park down the _____.
   street / corner

5. There are a bus stop and a _____ around the _____.
   subway station / laundry room   corner / basement

▶ Do it yourself!

**A. Personalization. Complete
the chart about your
neighborhood.**

**B. Pair work. Compare your
neighborhoods.**

Place	Location
a park	*down the street*
a convenience store	
a bus stop or subway station	
a school	
a _____	

In my neighborhood, there's
a subway station around
the corner.

Practical conversations

A. Listen and read.

A: I'm looking for an apartment in the neighborhood.

B: Well, there's a nice apartment on Beach Street.

A: How much is the rent?

B: $550 a month. Would you like to see it?

A: Yes. Can you show it to me today?

B. Listen again and repeat.

C. Pair work. Now use the for rent ads and your own words.

Other times

today
tonight
tomorrow morning

A: I'm looking for _____ in the neighborhood.

B: Well, there's a nice _____ on _____.

A: How much is the rent?

B: $_____ a month. Would you like to see it?

A: Yes. Can you show it to me _____?

A. Listen and read.

A: I have a few questions about the neighborhood.

B: Sure.

A: Is there a park nearby?

B: Yes, right around the corner.

A: And what about a bus stop or a subway station?

B: Yes, there's a bus stop across the street.

B. Listen again and repeat.

C. Pair work. **Now use the map and your <u>own</u> words.**

A: I have a few questions about the neighborhood.

B: _____.

A: Is there a _____ nearby?

B: Yes, right _____.

A: And what about a _____?

B: Yes, _____.

Model 3　Sign a lease.

A. **Listen and read.**

A: I'd like to rent the apartment.

B: OK. Here's the lease. Please read it carefully.

A: Thanks, I will. Is there anything else?

B: Yes. There's a security deposit. It's one month's rent—$550.

A: Can I give it to you tonight?

B: That's fine. No problem.

B. **Listen again and repeat.**

C. Pair work. **Choose an apartment or a house from the ads on page 20. Talk about the lease and security deposit. Use your <u>own</u> words.**

Rental Agreement

Term of lease: ___1 year___

Address: __33 Beach Street__

Rent: $550 per month　Security: ___$550___

A: I'd like to rent the _apa_____.

B: OK. Here's the lease. Please read it carefully.

A: __This__. Is there anything else?

B: Yes. There's a security deposit. It's one month's rent—$_____.

A: Can I give it to you __to____?

B: __fin____.

➤ Do it yourself!

With two classmates, create a conversation for the people.

**Ask about an apartment.
Talk about the neighborhood.**

➤ Practical grammar

Object pronouns it and them

A. **Complete each sentence with it or them.**

1. **A:** When did you rent your apartment?

    B: I rented _____ yesterday.
    <u>the apartment</u>

2. **A:** Who paid the rent?

    B: Yoko paid _____.
    <u>the rent</u>

3. **A:** Who fixed the elevator?

    B: I fixed _____.
    <u>the elevator</u>

4. **A:** When can I paint the bathroom and kitchen?

    B: Please paint _____ today.
    <u>the bathroom and kitchen</u>

5. **A:** I already cleaned the laundry room.

    B: You did? When did you clean _____ ?
    <u>the laundry room</u>

6. **A:** Where are the keys?

    B: Right here. Do you need _____?
    <u>the keys</u>

Placement of object pronouns

Give <u>this bill</u> **to her**. = Give <u>**it**</u> **to her**.

Please sign <u>this lease</u> **for me**. = Please sign <u>**it**</u> **for me**.

I'll give <u>these messages</u> **to her.** = I'll give <u>**them**</u> **to her**.

Pay <u>the rent</u> **for Mariana and me**. = Pay <u>**it**</u> **for us**.

22   Unit 2

B. Put the words in order. Write each sentence on the line.

1. They / for us / it / left / . _They left it for us._

2. Why / for her / it / are you cashing / ? _____

   _____

3. I'm going / it / for them / to pay / . _____

   _____

4. to us / them / Please / read / . _____

5. it / do / for me / Please / . _____

C. Write sentences with two object pronouns.

1. Please give the electric bill to Claire. _Please give it to her._

2. Please read the ads to Mr. Pinto. _____

   _____

3. Please ask the Kermians for the security deposit. _____

   _____

4. Please clean the basement with Susan and me. _____

   _____

➤ Do it yourself!

A. Give some of these things to your classmates. Complete the chart.

Item	Classmate
keys	Jose
1.	
2.	
3.	
4. Your own idea: _____	

keys

a wallet

a checkbook

a driver's license

B. Discussion. **Talk about what you did.**

What did you do with your keys?

I gave them to Jose.

Authentic practice 1

With words you know, YOU can talk to this apartment manager.

🎧 **A.** Listen and read.

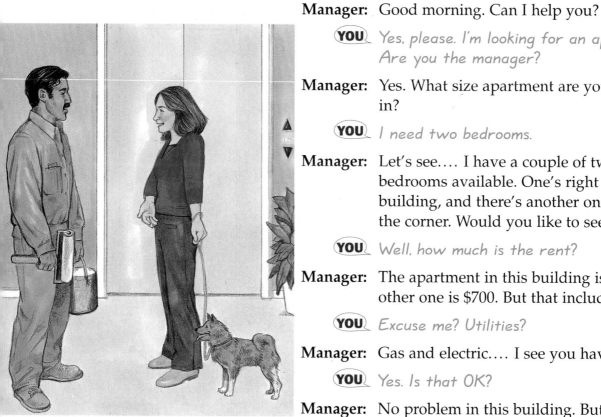

Manager: Good morning. Can I help you?

YOU Yes, please. I'm looking for an apartment. Are you the manager?

Manager: Yes. What size apartment are you interested in?

YOU I need two bedrooms.

Manager: Let's see…. I have a couple of two-bedrooms available. One's right here in this building, and there's another one around the corner. Would you like to see them?

YOU Well, how much is the rent?

Manager: The apartment in this building is $600. The other one is $700. But that includes utilities.

YOU Excuse me? Utilities?

Manager: Gas and electric…. I see you have a dog.

YOU Yes. Is that OK?

Manager: No problem in this building. But the one around the corner has a no-pet policy.

YOU I'd like to see the apartment in this building. Can you show it to me today?

🎧 **B.** Listen to the manager. Read _your_ part out loud.

🎧 **C.** Listen and read. Choose _your_ response. Circle the letter.

1. "Is a one-bedroom OK?"

   a. Yes, that's fine.   **b.** No. I have a dog.

2. "It's $900 a month, including utilities."

   a. What about gas and electric?   **b.** That's too expensive for us.

3. "I have a couple of two-bedrooms available."

   a. Can you show it to me today?   **b.** Can you show them to me today?

🎧 D. **Listen. Choose your response. Circle the letter.**

1. **a.** I need three bedrooms.　　　　　**b.** That's interesting.

2. **a.** Where is it?　　　　　　　　　　**b.** Can I see it tonight?

3. **a.** No problem. I have two dogs.　　**b.** That's OK.

Listening comprehension

🎧 A. **Listen to the conversation. Then write yes or no.**

1. The people are talking on the phone. _____

2. The people are talking about an apartment building. _____

🎧 B. **Read the questions. Then listen again for the answers. Circle the letter.**

1. When is the laundry room open?

   a. From Monday to Saturday.　　　**b.** Seven days a week.

2. When is the rent due?

   a. By the 10th of the month.　　　 **b.** By the 25th of the month.

3. How much is the late fee?

   a. $10.　　　　　　　　　　　　　**b.** $25.

🎧 C. **In your own words. Listen again. Answer the question and then talk with a partner.**

What's Mr. Azizi's problem and how does he solve it? _____

_____

➤ Do it yourself!

A. **Write your own response. Then read your conversation out loud with a partner.**

What size house are you interested in?

YOU _____

The security is one month's rent.

YOU _____

We have a no-pet policy. Is that OK?

YOU _____

B. **Personalization. Talk about the rules in your apartment or house.**

Reading

A. Read the questions. Then read the ads and answer the questions.

1. How many apartments are for rent? _____

2. How many houses are for rent? _____

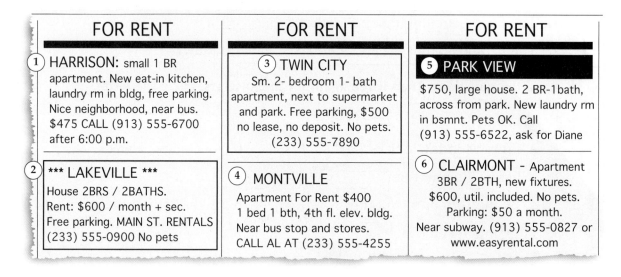

FOR RENT

(1) **HARRISON:** small 1 BR apartment. New eat-in kitchen, laundry rm in bldg, free parking. Nice neighborhood, near bus. $475 CALL (913) 555-6700 after 6:00 p.m.

(2) *** **LAKEVILLE** ***
House 2BRS / 2BATHS. Rent: $600 / month + sec. Free parking. MAIN ST. RENTALS (233) 555-0900 No pets

FOR RENT

(3) **TWIN CITY**
Sm. 2- bedroom 1- bath apartment, next to supermarket and park. Free parking, $500 no lease, no deposit. No pets. (233) 555-7890

(4) **MONTVILLE**
Apartment For Rent $400 1 bed 1 bth, 4th fl. elev. bldg. Near bus stop and stores. CALL AL AT (233) 555-4255

FOR RENT

(5) **PARK VIEW**
$750, large house. 2 BR-1bath, across from park. New laundry rm in bsmnt. Pets OK. Call (913) 555-6522, ask for Diane

(6) **CLAIRMONT** - Apartment 3BR / 2BTH, new fixtures. $600, util. included. No pets. Parking: $50 a month. Near subway. (913) 555-0827 or www.easyrental.com

B. Critical thinking. Read about the people. Which apartment or house is good for them? Write the number of the ad.

The Mees

1. Cynthia and Herman Mee want a one-bedroom apartment. They want to be near a bus stop. They can pay only $450 a month. _____

The Riveras

2. Hugo and Marta Rivera need an apartment or a house. They have two daughters, so they'd like two bedrooms and two bathrooms. They need parking for two cars. They can pay only $600 a month for rent and parking. _____

Farmer

3. Art Farmer and his son need a two-bedroom apartment. Mr. Farmer has a car, so he needs parking. _____

The Harrises

4. Wayne and Natasha Harris need a two-bedroom house or apartment. They have a dog. _____

26   Unit 2

Alvaro and Rosa Cordova need an apartment. They filled out a rental information form. Read their form and then fill out a rental form for yourself. Use your <u>own</u> information.

MAIN STREET RENTALS No fee to renter. You need it. We find it.

Name: <u>Alvaro and Rosa Cordova</u>   Phone: <u>(773) 555-6487</u>
Current Address: <u>7521 Western Avenue, Chicago, IL 60626</u>
Housing needs: ☐ House   ☑ Apartment
   bedrooms (number) <u>1</u>   bathrooms (number) <u>1</u>
   rent (maximum) $<u>400</u>
Desired location: <u>Chicago</u>   Neighborhood: <u>South Side</u>
Off-street parking needs: ☑ yes   ☐ no
Special needs: Check if important.
☐ pets   ☐ elevator   ☑ laundry room   ☐ bus/subway   ☐ parking

MAIN STREET RENTALS No fee to renter. You need it. We find it.

Name: _____   Phone: _____
Current Address: _____
Housing needs: ☐ House   ☐ Apartment
   bedrooms (number) _____   bathrooms (number) _____
   rent (maximum) $_____
Desired location: _____   Neighborhood: _____
Off-street parking needs: ☐ yes   ☐ no
Special needs: Check if important.
☐ pets   ☐ elevator   ☐ laundry room   ☐ bus/subway   ☐ parking

For extra practice, go to page 140.

> ## Do it yourself!   A plan-ahead project

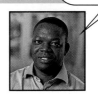

I like this apartment. It has two bedrooms.

A. **Pair work. Bring apartment ads from the newspaper to class. Find one or two apartments that are good for you. Talk about the ads.**

B. **Collaborative activity. Talk about your own apartment or house with a partner. Then write an ad for it.**

FOR RENT _____
_____
_____
_____
_____

➤ Review

A. **Vocabulary. Complete each sentence. Write the words on the line.**

1. My new apartment is on the ground floor. I won't need _____.

   an elevator / a convenience store

2. The park is right around _____.

   the street / the corner

3. The _____ is one month's rent—$745.

   security deposit / electric bill

B. **Conversation. Choose your response. Circle the letter.**

1. "What size apartment are you interested in?"

   a. We need two bedrooms and one bathroom.   **b.** We need to be near the subway.

2. "Here's your new lease."

   a. Thanks. I'll read it carefully.   **b.** Can I pay it tomorrow?

3. "There's a convenience store right around the corner."

   a. Is it nearby?   **b.** That's good.

C. **Grammar. Write sentences with two object pronouns.**

1. Please give the lease to John. _Please give it to him._

2. Please read the directions to Mrs. Tabor. _____

3. Please paint the bathroom for the Kermians. _____

4. Please clean the kitchen with Ellen and me. _____

D. **Reading. Read the ads. Read about the people. Which apartment or house is good for them? Write the number of the ad.**

1. Dennis and Fanny Tu need a two-bedroom house or apartment. They want two bathrooms. They can pay only $500 a month. _____

2. Ed Batista needs a two-bedroom house or apartment. He needs to be near a bus stop. He has a daughter, so he'd like to be near a school. _____

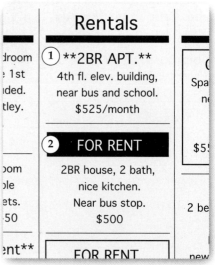

Rentals

droom 1) **2BR APT.**
e 1st   4th fl. elev. building,
ıded.   near bus and school.
tley. $525/month

2   FOR RENT
ɔom   2BR house, 2 bath,
le   nice kitchen.
ets.   Near bus stop.
-50 $500

ent**   FOR RENT

Spa
n

$5!

2 be

new

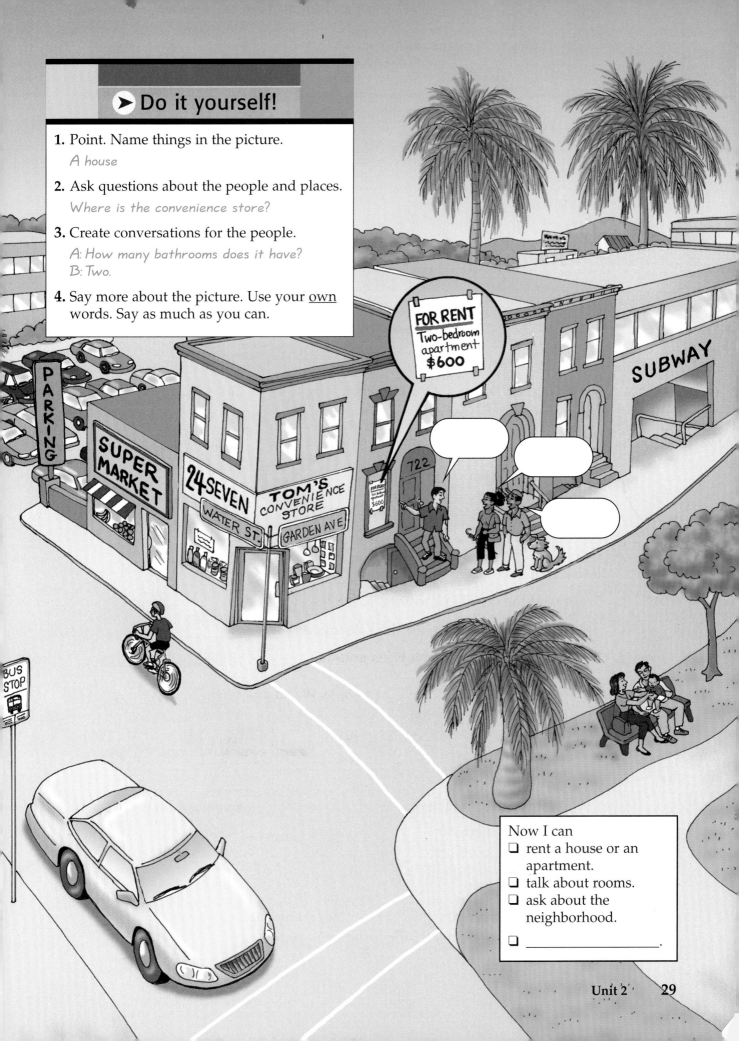

➤ Do it yourself!

1. Point. Name things in the picture.
   A house

2. Ask questions about the people and places.
   Where is the convenience store?

3. Create conversations for the people.
   A: How many bathrooms does it have?
   B: Two.

4. Say more about the picture. Use your <u>own</u> words. Say as much as you can.

Now I can
❑ rent a house or an apartment.
❑ talk about rooms.
❑ ask about the neighborhood.
❑ _____.

Your equipment and machines

▶ Vocabulary

Picture dictionary

🎧 A. Listen.

Cars and trucks

① a car	⑦ a new car	⑬ a tire
② an SUV	⑧ a used car	⑭ a door
③ a van	⑨ a headlight	⑮ a window
④ a truck	⑩ a hood	⑯ a trunk
⑤ a tow truck	⑪ an engine	⑰ a brake pedal
⑥ a pickup truck	⑫ windshield wipers	⑱ a gas pedal

Products for cars

⑲ gas
⑳ oil

Actions

㉑ remove
㉒ replace
㉓ check

Two-word verbs

㉔ drop off ㉕ pick up ㉖ turn on ㉗ turn off ㉘ fill up

🎧 **B.** Listen again and repeat.

🎧 **C.** Listen to the conversations. Then listen again and match each picture with a conversation. Write the letter on the line.

Conversation 1 _____   a.

Conversation 2 _____

Conversation 3 _____

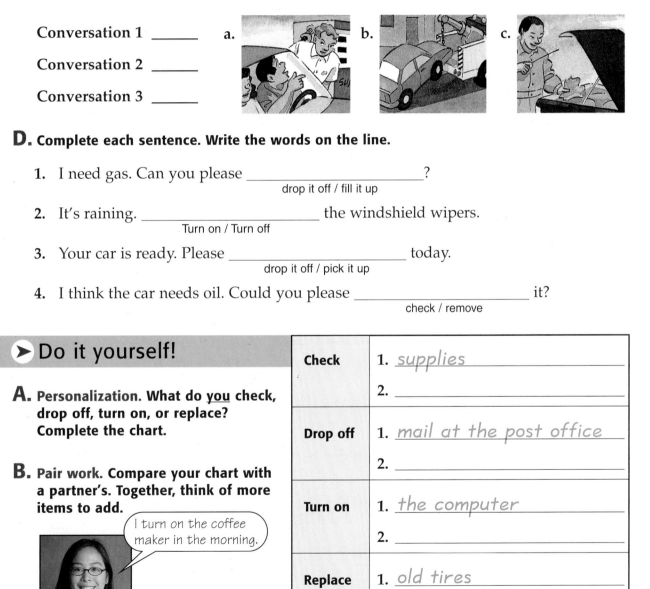

b.   c.

D. Complete each sentence. Write the words on the line.

1. I need gas. Can you please _____?
    <small>drop it off / fill it up</small>

2. It's raining. _____ the windshield wipers.
    <small>Turn on / Turn off</small>

3. Your car is ready. Please _____ today.
    <small>drop it off / pick it up</small>

4. I think the car needs oil. Could you please _____ it?
    <small>check / remove</small>

➤ **Do it yourself!**

A. Personalization. What do **you** check, drop off, turn on, or replace? Complete the chart.

B. Pair work. Compare your chart with a partner's. Together, think of more items to add.

> I turn on the coffee maker in the morning.

Check	1. _supplies_
	2. _____
Drop off	1. _mail at the post office_
	2. _____
Turn on	1. _the computer_
	2. _____
Replace	1. _old tires_
	2. _____

Model 1   Describe a problem with a machine. Ask for an estimate.

🎧 **A.** Listen and read.

A: The door won't open.
B: No problem. Can you leave it here?
   You can pick it up at about five.
A: OK. Can you give me an estimate?
B: Sure. It'll be about $50.

🎧 **B.** Listen again and repeat.

🎧 **Mechanical problems**

won't open	won't go off
won't close	won't start
won't go on	

C. Pair work. **Describe a problem. Ask for an estimate.
Use the words in the box or your <u>own</u> words.**

A: The _____ won't _____.
B: _____. Can you leave it here? You can
   pick it up at about _____.
A: OK. Can you give me an estimate?
B: _____. It'll be about _____.

headlights	door	window
trunk	hood	engine

Model 2   Report a problem and schedule a repair.

🎧 **A.** Listen and read.

A: Auto Repair. Tony speaking.
B: Hello. I have a problem. My
   windshield wipers aren't working.
A: What kind of car is it?
B: A Monsoon SUV.
A: OK. Can you drop it off at about 10:00?
B: Yes. That's good for me.

🎧 **B.** Listen again and repeat.

🎧 **Problems**

not working
making a funny
      sound

Gareek!

C. Pair work. **Now use the pictures or your <u>own</u> words.**

A: Auto Repair. _____ speaking.
B: _____. I have a problem. My _____.
A: What kind of car is it?
B: _____.
A: OK. Can you drop it off at about _____?
B: _____.

a horn   a radio

a turn signal

Model 3   Leave a car for a repair.

🎧 **A. Listen and read.**

A: I'm here to drop off my car.
B: What's the problem?
A: Well, I was driving to work, and my oil pressure warning light went on.
B: OK, I can check it for you.
A: Great! What time can I pick it up?
B: I'm not sure. I'll give you a call.

🎧 **B. Listen again and repeat.**

C. Pair work. **Leave a car, van, or truck for repair. Use the picture and your <u>own</u> words.**

A: I'm here to drop off my _____.
B: What's the problem?
A: Well, I was driving to _____, and my _____ warning light went on.
B: OK, I can check it for you.
A: _____! What time can I pick it up?
B: _____. I'll give you a call.

Engine warning light	🔧	**Check Engine!**
Oil pressure warning light	🛢	**Oil Pressure!**
Brake fluid warning light	◎	**Brake Fluid!**

➤ Do it yourself!

A. Pair work. **Create a conversation about a repair. Use the pictures or your <u>own</u> machine.**

a TV   a VCR

What's the problem? Repairs FREE ESTIMATES

The door won't open.

B. Present your conversation to the class.

Practical grammar

It and them with two-word verbs

Review: One-word verbs

This door won't close. Can you **fix it**?

Two-word verbs

We can't fix your car today. Please **drop it off** tomorrow.

A. Review. **Complete each sentence with it or them.**

1. The windshield wipers aren't working. Please check _____.

2. The window won't open. Can she replace _____?

3. I can't change these tires. Will you change _____ for me?

4. The headlights won't go on. Is he going to fix _____?

B. Put the underlined words in order. Write each sentence on the line.

1. The windshield wipers aren't working. can't / I / on / them / turn /.

   *I can't turn them on.*_____

2. My car needs new tires. it / Can / off / drop / I / later /?

   _____

3. I have to turn on the headlights. button / on / turns / them / Which /?

   _____

4. I'd like to pick up my car today. up / can / I / pick / it / What time /?

   _____

5. I need gas. Please / it / fill / up /.

   _____

The past continuous

What's wrong?

I **wasn't driving** a new car.
Was she **driving** an SUV?   Yes, she **was**.
Who **was driving** the car?   I **was**.
What kind of car **were** they **driving**?   A Monsoon van.

Well, I **was driving** to work, and my oil pressure warning light went on.

C. Complete the paragraph with the past continuous. Write the words on the line.

Ann Del Rio's SUV _____ a funny sound, and she wanted a mechanic to check
                        1. make

her car. But Marcus _____ the oil in a customer's used van. Antonio _____
                        2. change   3. replace

the headlights. Josef _____ the engine, and Donna _____ the old tires.
                        4. fix   5. remove

Even Al, the manager, was busy. He _____ on the phone.
                                        6. talk

The past continuous and the simple past tense

The past continuous shows an action that continued in the past.
The simple past tense shows an action that happened once and then stopped.
  past continuous   simple past tense

I **was eating** lunch when she **called**.

D. Choose the past continuous or the simple past tense. Write the verb on the line.

Yesterday I _____ the car ads in the newspaper when my sister
                1. read / was reading

_____. She _____ me what I _____, and I
2. called / was calling   3. asked / was asking   4. did / was doing

_____ her. So after work, she _____ with me to a used car lot.
5. told / was telling   6. went / was going

The manager of the lot _____ us a nice car, and I _____ it!
                            7. showed / was showing   8. bought / was buying

➤ Do it yourself!

What were you doing at 10:00 this morning?

I was eating breakfast.

A. Pair work. Ask your partner questions beginning with "What were you doing?" Use these times.

`10:00`   `9:00`

This morning   Yesterday

B. Discussion. Tell the class what your partner was doing.

Authentic practice 1

With words you know, YOU can talk to this driver.

🎧 **A.** **Listen and read.**

Driver: Bad news. Van 13 won't start.

YOU *Van 13? Really? It was working this morning.*

Driver: I know. It started fine. But when I was leaving the parking lot, it just stopped. Right in the middle of the exit.

YOU *Excuse me? Where?*

Driver: In the exit. I called maintenance. They're working on it now. But I need to pick up 18 kids. I'm already late.

YOU *No problem. You can have van 4. Emil dropped it off at noon.*

Driver: Great. Where can I pick it up?

YOU *Outside. Next to the door. Here are the keys.*

Driver: Thanks. I owe you one.

🎧 **B.** **Listen to the driver. Read your part out loud.**

🎧 **C.** **Listen and read. Choose your response. Circle the letter.**

1. "Bad news."

   a. What's the problem?   b. Can I give them to you tomorrow?

2. "Where can I drop it off?"

   a. I'll give you an estimate.   b. At Tony's Auto Repair.

3. "Thanks. I owe you one."

   a. Please give me two.   b. You're welcome.

🎧 **D.** **Listen. Choose your response. Circle the letter.**

1. a. Oh, no.   b. Turn it off.

2. a. What time is Marie going to drop it off? b. That's great. Thanks.

3. a. I don't know. It was working yesterday. b. No problem.

A. Listen to the conversation. Then listen again and answer the questions. Circle the letter.

1. Where are the people?

   a. At home.   **b.** In a repair shop.

2. What's the problem?

   a. The VCR doesn't work.   **b.** The repair is too expensive.

B. Listen to the conversation again. Check ☑ yes, no, or I don't know.

	yes	no	I don't know
1. She wants to buy a new VCR.	❏	❏	❏
2. The VCR was working this morning.	❏	❏	❏
3. He can fix the VCR.	❏	❏	❏
4. She has to drop off the VCR tomorrow.	❏	❏	❏
5. He gave her an estimate.	❏	❏	❏
6. She'll call him tomorrow.	❏	❏	❏

C. In your own words. Listen again. Answer the questions and then talk with a partner.

1. What's the problem? _____

2. What is the customer going to do? _____

➤ Do it yourself!

A. Write your own response. Then read your conversation out loud with a partner.

What's the problem with the TV?

YOU _____

Well, I can take a look at it this afternoon. OK?

YOU _____

Can you give me a number where I can call you with an estimate?

YOU _____

B. Personalization. Talk about a problem with your own vehicle or machine.

Authentic practice 2

Reading

A. Look at the owner's manual. Read the instructions.

UNIVERSAL S2500   **WARNING LIGHTS**

UNLEADED FUEL ONLY

Low fuel warning light Get gas now!

Brake fluid warning light Stop immediately, open the hood, and check the brake fluid. If it is below the MIN mark, do not drive. Tow the truck to an authorized Universal dealer for service.

Generator warning light Check battery.

Oil pressure warning light Do not drive! Tow truck to nearest authorized Universal dealer for service.

Bulb failure warning light Check bulbs. Replace them if necessary.

page 12

B. Critical thinking. **Look at the three warning lights. These people were driving their Universal pickup trucks when the warning lights went on. What do they have to do? Circle the letter.**

Lim

1. Ms. Lim has to _____.

   a. fill the car with gas

   b. check the brake fluid

Montoya

2. Mr. Montoya has to _____.

   a. stop driving and tow his truck to the dealer

   b. replace the bulb

Baraf

3. Ms. Baraf has to _____.

   a. replace the bulb

   b. stop driving and check the battery

38   Unit 3

A. Read Ms. Lim's repair order at the Universal Truck dealership. Answer the questions.

UNIVERSAL CARS AND TRUCKS	Repair/Service Work Order
Describe problem	**NAME** Connie Lim / **DATE** April 2, 2002
I was driving to work and the brake fluid light came on.	**ADDRESS** 3601 North Highway / San Antonio TX 78202
	PHONE NUMBER (210) 555-3766
	MODEL AND YEAR 330 Super Pickup 1999 / **LICENSE PLATE NUMBER** G45 OKJ

Estimate	**Drop-off time**	**Pick-up time**
$85 00	8:20 a.m.	4:30 p.m. (will call)

1. What is the model name of Ms. Lim's truck? _____

2. When will her truck be ready? _____

B. Collaborative activity. **Create a conversation with a partner. Then fill out the repair order together.**

Partner A: You have a 2001 Monsoon SUV, license plate CO 3241.
You were driving home from work when the oil pressure warning light came on.

Partner B: You work at the Monsoon repair shop.

DESCRIPTION OF PROBLEM	*Monsoon* Cars and Trucks 7242
	REPAIR/SERVICE WORK ORDER
	NAME / **DATE**
	ADDRESS
ESTIMATE	
	PHONE NUMBER / **LICENSE PLATE NUMBER**
	MODEL AND YEAR
	DROP-OFF TIME
TOTAL	**PICK-UP TIME**

For extra practice, go to page 141.

> ● Do it yourself! A plan-ahead project

Discussion. Bring in a manual for a car or for a machine or use the one here. Talk about the warnings.

Do not spill liquids on the machine.

Do not use any appliance with a damaged cord or plug.

Review

A. Vocabulary. Complete each sentence. Write the words on the line.

1. My car won't start. I need a _____.
   <u>tow truck / pickup truck</u>

2. There's a problem with the _____. I can't close it.
   <u>engine / trunk</u>

3. It's a good idea to _____ the oil when you buy gas.
   <u>remove / check</u>

B. Conversation. Choose <u>your</u> response. Circle the letter.

1. "Can you bring it in today?"

   a. Sure. What time?   **b.** Yes. I can leave it here.

2. "Can she leave it a while?"

   a. I think so. I'll check.   **b.** Next to the exit door.

3. "It'll be about $200."

   a. Can you give me an estimate?   **b.** That's a lot. I'll have to think about it.

C. Grammar. Put the underlined words in order. Write each sentence on the line.

1. We dropped our car off this morning.   <u>pick / What time / up / it / we / can /?</u>

   _____

2. Her headlights aren't working.   <u>on / She / them / can't / turn / .</u>

   _____

D. Grammar. Choose the past continuous or the simple past tense. Circle the verb.

Dear Lisa:

It <u>rained / was raining</u> yesterday, and I <u>drove / was driving</u> my old pickup truck.
    1.   2.

At 3:00 my problems <u>started / were starting</u>. The windshield wipers
                            3.

<u>stopped / were stopping</u>, and I couldn't see. And then the oil pressure warning
    4.

light <u>went on / was going on</u>. The owner's manual for the truck <u>said / was saying</u>
        5.   6.

to stop right away. While I <u>read / was reading</u> the manual, a friend
                   7.

<u>saw / was seeing</u> me. That was lucky! She <u>drove / was driving</u> me to a telephone,
  8.   9.

and I <u>called / was calling</u> a tow truck. What a day!
      10.

> **Do it yourself!**

1. Point. Name things in the picture.

  A tow truck

2. Talk about the people.

  She's dropping off her car.

3. Create conversations for the people.

  A: What's the problem?
  B: The headlights aren't working.

4. Say more about the picture. Use your <u>own</u> words. Say as much as you can.

Now I can
❑ report problems with vehicles or machines.
❑ request service or repair.
❑ ask for an estimate.
❑ understand warnings.
❑ _____ .

Your customers

Objectives
- talk about personal care products and medicines
- request and offer a rain check
- discuss an overcharge

Vocabulary

Picture dictionary

A. Listen.

Personal care products		Medicines	Other words	
(1) soap	(6) a comb	(10) painkillers	(12) a drugstore	(17) a price
(2) shampoo	(7) a brush	(11) cough medicine	(13) a camera	(18) a sale price
(3) toothpaste	(8) a thermometer		(14) film	(19) dirty
(4) a toothbrush	(9) tissues		(15) a hair dryer	(20) clean
(5) deodorant			(16) a brand	

Personal care

㉑ Wash your hair. ㉒ Brush your hair. ㉓ Comb your hair. ㉔ Brush your teeth.

B. Listen again and repeat.

C. Listen to the conversations. Then listen again and match each picture with a conversation. Write the letter on the line.

Conversation 1 _____

Conversation 2 _____

Conversation 3 _____

a.

b.

c.

D. Complete each sentence. Write the words on the line.

1. What kind of _____ do you take for a headache? I take aspirin.

painkiller / cough medicine

2. Where's my _____? I want to take a picture of you.

camera / thermometer

3. I have to wash my hair. Do we have any of that great _____?

deodorant / shampoo

4. What brand of _____ do you want for your camera?

tissues / film

5. This brush is _____. I'm going to wash it.

dirty / clean

➤ **Do it yourself!**

A. Personalization. Make a list of things **you** buy at the drugstore.

B. Pair work. Compare your list with a partner's. Do you buy the same things?

What do you buy at the drugstore?

Personal care products	Medicines and other things
1.	1.
2.	2.
3.	3.
4.	4.

Practical conversations

A. Listen and read.

A: I'm looking for a hair dryer. How much is the one over here?

B: Which one?

A: The red one.

B: $24.99.

A: Do you have any cheaper ones?

B: Yes. And they're on sale. They're only $9.99. They're usually $14.99.

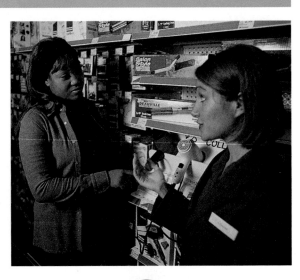

B. Listen again and repeat.

C. Pair work. **Now use the pictures or your own words.**

A: I'm looking for _____. How much is the one over here?

B: Which one?

A: The _____ one.

B: $ _____.

A: Do you have any cheaper ones?

B: Yes. And they're on sale. They're only _____. They're usually _____.

A. Listen and read.

A: That'll be $7.21, please.

B: But this film's on sale for $4.99.

A: I'm sorry, but that price is for the store brand. And we're sold out.

B: That's too bad. Will you give me a rain check?

A: No problem. Here you go. It's good for a month.

B. Listen again and repeat.

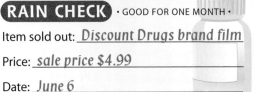

RAIN CHECK · GOOD FOR ONE MONTH ·

Item sold out: _Discount Drugs brand film_

Price: _sale price $4.99_

Date: _June 6_

C. Pair work. **Now use the pictures or your <u>own</u> words.**

> **A:** That'll be $ _____ , please.
>
> **B:** But this _____ 's on sale for $ _____ .
>
> **A:** I'm sorry, but that price is for the store brand. And we're sold out.
>
> **B:** That's too bad. Will you give me a rain check?
>
> **A:** _____ . Here you go. It's good for _____ .

Model 3   Talk about an overcharge. Offer to correct it.

A. **Listen and read.**

> **A:** Excuse me. I think I was overcharged. This shampoo's on sale.
>
> **B:** Oh, I'm sorry. Let me have a look.
>
> **A:** See, it says "Special $1.99."
>
> **B:** Yes, you're right. I'll ring it up again.

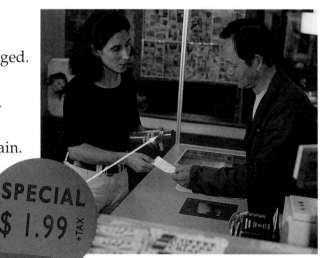

B. **Listen again and repeat.**

C. Pair work. **Now use your <u>own</u> words.**

> **A:** Excuse me. I think I was overcharged. This _____ 's on sale.
>
> **B:** Oh, I'm sorry. Let me have a look.
>
> **A:** See, it says "_____ ."
>
> **B:** _____ . I'll ring it up again.

➤ **Do it yourself!**

Pair work. **Create a conversation for the people in the picture. Use your <u>own</u> words.**

Practical grammar

Comparisons with adjectives: comparatives

The small cameras are **cheaper than** the big cameras.

cheap	cheap**er**	nice	nicer	busy	bus**ier**	hot	hot**ter**
new	new**er**			early	earl**ier**		
old	old**er**			dirty	dirt**ier**		
clean	clean**er**						

I like Clean Skin soap.

I like it too, but it's **more expensive than** the store brand.

expensive	**more expensive**
beautiful	**more beautiful**

Discount Drugs shampoo is **better than** Cheapway.

Yes, but it's more expensive.

good	**better**
bad	**worse**

A. Complete each sentence with the comparative form of the adjective.

1. Is Clean Skin soap _____*better*_____ than the store brand?
   good

2. Our camera is _____ than their camera.
   new

3. Today's weather is _____ than yesterday's weather!
   bad

4. A computer is usually _____ than a cash register.
   expensive

5. Are the cashiers _____ today than they were yesterday?
   busy

B. Write comparisons with the words.

1. Bell Food Store is / cheap / Quickway

   Bell Food Store is cheaper than Quickway.

2. My new camera is / large / my old camera

   _____

46   Unit 4

3. Discount Drugs is / clean / Quickway

_____

4. The large hair dryers are / expensive / the small hair dryers

_____

5. Today's weather is / hot / yesterday's weather

_____

One / ones and questions with Which

C. **Complete each conversation with <u>Which</u>, <u>one</u>, or <u>ones</u>.**

1. **A:** _Which_ comb did you buy?

   B: The black one.

2. **A:** _____ toothbrushes do you like?

   B: I like the cheaper ones.

3. **A:** _____ deodorant is on sale?

   B: The larger one.

4. **A:** Is she buying the red cough medicine?

   B: No, she's buying the orange _____.

5. **A:** Do they like these new thermometers?

   B: No. They like the old _____.

6. **A:** Which tissues do you want?

   B: The _____ over there.

7. **A:** Why did you sell your old camera?

   B: I bought a better _____.

8. **A:** Why did you use this shampoo?

   B: Because it's better than that _____.

➤ Do it yourself!

A. **Personalization. Complete the chart with three things you buy at the drugstore.**

B. **Pair work. Compare brands.**

Product	Brand	Adjective
soap	So Soft	cheap
1.		
2.		
3.		

With words you know, YOU can talk to this customer.

🎧 **A.** **Listen and read.**

Customer: Excuse me. Do you work here?

YOU *Yes. I'm the assistant manager. Can I help you?*

Customer: I hope so. I bought this here last Saturday, but there's something wrong with it.

YOU *Oh, that's too bad. What's wrong?*

Customer: The film compartment won't close. Can I exchange it?

YOU *I'm sorry. We're sold out right now. Would you like a rain check?*

Customer: Well, that's very nice of you, but I think I'd like to have another brand. How much are those?

YOU *Well, those are on sale—only $20. And they're better than this one, I think.*

Customer: Terrific. I'll take one.

🎧 **B.** **Listen to the customer. Read _your_ part out loud.**

🎧 **C.** **Listen and read. Choose _your_ response. Circle the letter.**

1. "Excuse me. Do you work here?"

    a. No, I'm sorry, I don't.   **b.** It doesn't work. I want to exchange it.

2. "There's something wrong with this camera."

    a. OK, I'll ring it up again.   **b.** Oh, what's wrong with it?

3. "I'd like to exchange this for one that's on sale."

    a. Sure. We're sold out.   **b.** Fine. We have one for only $10.00.

4. "How much is this soap?"

    a. I'll take three boxes.   **b.** It's on sale for $1.29.

5. "I'll take one."

    a. Here you go.   **b.** That's too bad.

🎧 **D.** **Listen. Choose your response. Circle the letter.**

1. **a.** No problem.   **b.** No. It's too expensive.

2. **a.** Two months.   **b.** We're sold out.

3. **a.** I can give you a rain check.   **b.** Let me look at your receipt.

Listening comprehension

🎧 **A.** **Listen to the announcement. Then answer the questions. Circle the letter.**

1. Who is the speaker?

   a. an announcer on the radio   **b.** a customer of 77 Electronics

2. What is 77 Electronics?

   a. a brand of camera   **b.** a store

3. What is the speaker talking about?

   a. a copy shop   **b.** a sale

🎧 **B.** **Look at the chart. Then listen again for the price of each item. Write the prices on the chart.**

🎧 **C.** **In your own words. Listen again.**

What would you like to buy at 77 Electronics?

_____

Tell your partner why.

Item	Price
Perfect Picture camera	$ 27.77
Brew Right coffee maker	
Copy Clean home copier	
copier paper	
computer diskettes	
pocket calendar	

➤ Do it yourself!

A. **Write your own response. Then read your conversation out loud with a partner.**

Excuse me. Do you work here?   (YOU) _____

I have a problem.   (YOU) _____

I think I was overcharged for this camera.   (YOU) _____

B. **Personalization. Talk about a sale in your neighborhood.**

Reading

A. Read the ad. Check ☑ the items that are on sale.

❏ screwdrivers
❏ pliers
❏ drills
❏ saws
❏ goggles
❏ batteries

B. Critical thinking. **Read about these Tool Box customers. Choose the correct response.**

Yes, you're right. I'll ring that up for you again.

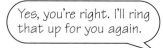

No, I'm sorry. That is the right price.

Walker

1. On Monday, Ms. Walker paid $2.99 for an 8' vinyl tape measure. She said to the cashier, "I think I was overcharged."

   Response: _____

Reyes

2. Ms. Reyes bought a 15" Rapid Cut saw on Tuesday. She paid $14.39. She checked her receipt and said to the cashier, "I think I was overcharged."

   Response: _____

Cheng

3. Mr. Cheng bought a Tool Box power drill on Wednesday. He paid $59.99. He said to the cashier, "I think I was overcharged."

   Response: _____

A. Look at the ad on page 50 again. Then look at the rain check from the Tool Box. Answer the question.

Late Monday afternoon, the power drills were sold out, so customers got rain checks. How long is the rain check good for? _____

_____

🔨 **The Tool Box**   **Rain Check**

Date _____ *September 18* _____

Sold-out item ___ *Tool Box power drill* ___

Sale price _____ *$42.99* _____

Good until _____ *October 18* _____

B. Collaborative activity. Create a conversation. It's Tuesday afternoon at the Tool Box. The power drills and the 26" saws are sold out.

Partner A, you are a customer. You want to buy a 26" saw. Ask Partner B for a rain check.

Partner B, you are a cashier. Fill out a rain check for Partner A.

🔨 **The Tool Box**   **Rain Check**

Date _____

Sold-out item _____

Sale price _____

Good until _____

For extra practice, go to page 142.

➤ **Do it yourself!**   A plan-ahead project

Discussion. Bring in ads from the newspaper or from stores in your neighborhood. Compare your ads.

Perfect Picture cameras are on sale at Discount Drugs for $19.99.

➤ Review

A. Vocabulary. Complete each sentence. Write the words on the line.

1. I'll be ready in a minute. I just have to _____ my teeth.
   brush / comb

2. I washed my hair with this _____, but I don't like it.
   toothpaste / shampoo

3. My hair is _____. I have to wash it.
   clean / dirty

B. Conversation. Choose your response. Circle the letter.

1. "We're sold out."

   a. Oh, that's too bad.   **b.** Is it good for a month?

2. "Excuse me. I think I was overcharged."

   a. OK. I'll give you a rain check.   **b.** Let me have a look at the price.

3. "I'm sorry. I'll ring it up again."

   a. Thanks.   **b.** That's worse.

C. Grammar. Complete each sentence with one or ones.

1. I need a new camera. How much is this _____?

2. Which toothbrushes are on sale? The _____ on the shelf?

3. Do you want these tissues or the _____ over there?

D. Grammar. Write comparisons with the words.

1. The Efficiency saw is / good / the Tool Box saw

   _____

2. I am / busy / my manager

   _____

E. Reading and writing.
Read the ad. Then fill out a rain check for one of the products.

$1.29 Quick Dry deodorant

Great Hair shampoo 2 bottles for $1.69

$.39 Clear & Fresh soap

Specials: May 22 only | Personal Products *Plus*

RAIN CHECK • good for one month •

Date: _____

Item: _____

Sale price: _____

Good until: _____

52   Unit 4

Your time

Objectives
- ask about schedules
- explain lateness
- read bus and train schedules
- buy tickets and pay fares

Vocabulary

Picture dictionary

Union–Chester
MTA Metro–South Railroad · Subject to tariff regulations · Good for travel between stations shown MTA Metro–South Railroad
Fare $4.00

Union–Chester   Chester – Union
MTA Metro–South Railroad · Subject to tariff regulations · Good for travel between stations shown MTA Metro–South Railroad
Fare $7.50

South St. - North End **EXPRESS**
45th Street
South Street   North End

South St. - North End **LOCAL**
15th Street   45th Street   North End
South Street   30th Street   60th Street

Before 8:00   After 8:00
6:00 7:00 8:00 9:00 10:00

A. Listen.

Transportation and commuting

				Other words
① leave	⑥ buy a ticket	⑪ be stuck in traffic	⑯ the express	⑱ before
② arrive	⑦ buy a token	⑫ run out of gas	⑰ the local	⑲ after
③ take a bus	⑧ use a fare card	⑬ the fare		
④ take a train	⑨ miss the bus	⑭ one way		
⑤ take a taxi	⑩ have a flat tire	⑮ round trip		

Ways to say the time

(20) three ten
ten after three
ten after
ten past three
ten past

(21) three fifteen
a quarter after three
a quarter after
a quarter past three
a quarter past

🎧 **How to say it**

present	past
leave	left
take	took
buy	bought
have	had
be	was / were

(22) three thirty
half past three
half past

(23) three forty-five
a quarter to four
a quarter to

🎧 **B.** Listen again and repeat.

🎧 **C.** Listen to the conversations. Then listen again and match each clock with a conversation. Write the letter on the line.

a.   b.   c.   d.   e.

1. _____   2. _____   3. _____   4. _____   5. _____

D. Complete the paragraph with words from the box.

took   missed   had   fare   bought   arrived   stuck in traffic   one-way ticket

What a day! First I was _____ for 20 minutes and then I
                                                          1.

_____ a flat tire! I _____ the 8:00 train, so I _____ the 9:35.
        2.   3.   4.

The round-trip _____ is $6.00. I had only $5.00, so I _____
                          5.   6.

a _____ . I _____ at work at 10:30 — one and a half hours late.
            7.   8.

➤ Do it yourself!

A. Personalization. What public transportation do **you** use? Complete the chart.

B. Discussion. Talk about the public transportation in your city or town. Is it good or bad? Expensive or cheap?

I take the subway to work. It's cheap, but it's dirty.

	Fare	Fare card, token, ticket, or cash?
bus	$1.50	fare card
bus		
subway		
train		

Model 1 Buy a ticket.

🎧 **A. Listen and read.**

A: One ticket to San Pedro, please.

B: Round trip or one way?

A: Round trip. What's the fare?

B: $2.50.

A: Here you go. When's the next train?

B: In 10 minutes. At 8:15.

🎧 **B. Listen again and repeat.**

C. Pair work. Now use the clock and the schedule and your _own_ words.

A: _____ to _____, please.

B: Round trip or one way?

A: _____. What's the fare?

B: _____.

A: Here you go. When's the next train?

B: In _____ minutes. At _____.

FROM DENSON TO SAN PEDRO

Monday to Friday

FARE	Denson - Carson	$3.85
	Denson - San Pedro	$4.25

LEAVE	ARRIVE	ARRIVE
Denson	**Carson**	**San Pedro**
5:12	5:24	5:31
5:22	5:34	5:41
5:32	5:44	5:51

Model 2 Ask about a bus or a train.

🎧 **A. Listen and read.**

A: Did the bus to Pleasantville leave yet?

B: Yes. You just missed it. It left five minutes ago.

A: Oh, no. When's the next one?

B: Well, they leave every 15 minutes, so you could take the 3:15.

🎧 **B. Listen again and repeat.**

C. Pair work. **Invent a bus or train to your <u>own</u> city or town.**

A: Did the _____ to _____ leave yet?

B: Yes. You just missed it. It left _____ ago.

A: Oh, no. When's the next one?

B: Well, they leave every _____, so you could take the _____.

Model 3   Ask if you're too late.

🎧 **A. Listen and read.**

A: Can I still make the 5:22?

B: Yes. It's still here. Do you need a ticket?

A: No, I already have one.

B: It's leaving soon. You should hurry.

🎧 **B. Listen again and repeat.**

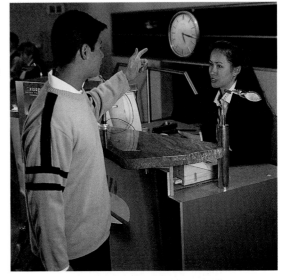

C. Pair work. **Now use the schedule and your <u>own</u> words.**

A: Can I still make the _____?

B: Yes. It's still here. Do you need a ticket?

A: _____.

B: It's leaving _____. You should hurry.

LEAVES	ARRIVES
9:05	10:00
9:15	10:10
9:25	10:20

➤ Do it yourself!

Pair work. **Create a conversation for the people in the picture. Use your <u>own</u> words.**

Practical grammar

Should

> Which train **should** I **take**?

> Metro South Line

> You **should take** the 6:15. It's an express.

Should I **take** the 5:12?	No, you **shouldn't**. You **should take** the 4:59.
Should he **buy** a one-way ticket?	Yes, he **should**.
When **should** I **arrive**?	How about ten to three?

A. Complete each sentence with a form of **should** and the verb.

1. He _should take_ the express. The local arrives too late.
   take

2. You _____ early tonight. There's a lot of traffic.
   leave

3. Which bus _____ we _____?
   take

4. Where _____ I _____ a token?
   buy

5. We _____ him before noon. He's very busy.
   call

6. You _____ the express. It doesn't stop at 79th Street.
   not take

7. Should they drive? No, they _____. They'll get stuck in traffic.
   should not

Could

> Which train should he take? He has to arrive before 9:30.

> Well, he **could take** the 8:25 local. Or he **could take** the 8:35 express.

Could I **take** the train?	The train already left, but you **could take** a taxi.
Could we **take** the bus?	No, you **couldn't**. It doesn't stop there.

B. Complete the conversations. Use a form of <u>could</u> and the verb.

Did the 7:55 express leave yet?

Yes, but you _____ the
1. take
local. It leaves at 8:03.

Bob missed the school bus again. What should we do?

Well, we _____
2. drive
him to school.

Or he _____!
3. walk

Which trains _____ we
_____ to get there
4. take
before 6:00?

Well, we _____
5. take
the 5:35 local.

No, we _____. It'll arrive
6. could not
too late. But look! We _____

still _____ the 5:22 express.
7. make

You're right. But we should hurry. It's leaving soon.

► Do it yourself!

**Pair work. Linda and Edward Kim are at Central Station. They work in Oak Plains. Work begins at 9:00. They have to arrive before 9:00 to be on time for work.
What trains could they take? What train should they take? Talk with a partner.**

The Kims

CARMEL LINE

Blue numbers = Express trains

Cent. Sta.	Northway	Hot Springs	Oak Plains	Carmel
7:15	7:30	8:00	8:30	9:00
7:25	7:40	--------	8:25	8:55
7:30	-------	8:05	--------	8:55
7:30	7:45	8:15	8:45	9:15
7:50	8:05	8:35	9:05	9:35

Authentic practice 1

With words you know, YOU can talk to this supervisor.

🎧 **A.** Listen and read.

Supervisor: Martina Loyola.

YOU *Ms. Loyola? Hi, this is Erika Bender. I'm sorry. I'm going to be late today.*

Supervisor: Are you OK, Erika? What's wrong?

YOU *Well, I had a flat tire. Then I missed my train. It left five minutes ago.*

Supervisor: That's too bad. I'm afraid you might miss the computer training class. It starts at nine sharp and it's already twenty to. You should take a taxi.

YOU *Excuse me?*

Supervisor: Could you take a taxi? It's already twenty minutes to nine.

YOU *Yes, I could.*

Supervisor: Good. Well, thanks for calling, Erika. Please hurry in.

YOU *OK, Ms. Loyola. See you soon.*

🎧 **B.** Listen to the supervisor. Read <u>your</u> part out loud.

🎧 **C.** Listen and read. Choose <u>your</u> response. Circle the letter.

1. "I'm afraid you might miss the 7:18."

   a. That's good.   **b.** When's the next one?

2. "The train leaves at 9:45 sharp."

   a. We should hurry.   **b.** Round trip or one way?

3. "I'm afraid you just missed the meeting."

   a. Oh, no!   **b.** It already left.

🎧 **D.** Listen. Choose <u>your</u> response. Circle the letter.

1. **a.** What's the problem?   **b.** Patrick? Hi.

2. **a.** I just missed it.   **b.** Yes. I'll take the next train.

3. **a.** OK. Thanks.   **b.** Oh, no. Did I miss it?

A. Listen to the conversation. Then answer the questions. Circle the letter.

1. Who are the people?

   a. A delivery driver and a customer.   **b.** A delivery driver and a co-worker.

2. What's the problem?

   a. A driver's stuck in traffic.   **b.** A driver's going to be late.

B. Listen again for the times. Circle the times.

1. What time is it?   `6:30` `6:45` `7:00` `7:15`

2. What time does Daniel's shift usually start?   `6:30` `6:45` `7:00` `7:15`

3. When will Miguel arrive at the Full Moon Diner?   `6:30` `6:45` `7:00` `7:15`

C. Critical thinking. Now listen again. When did the truck arrive at the company? Circle the time.   `6:30` `6:45` `7:00` `7:15`

D. In your own words. Listen again. Answer the question and then talk with a partner.

What is Daniel going to do? _____

➤ Do it yourself!

A. Write your <u>own</u> response. Then read your conversation out loud with a partner.

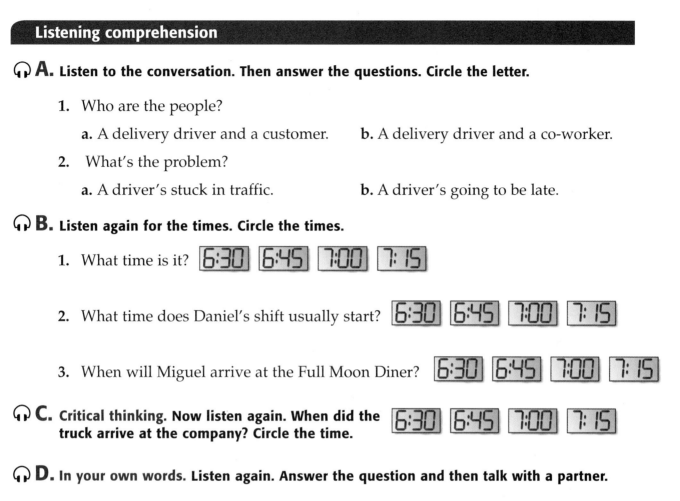

It's already twenty after nine. You're really late. Where are you?

YOU _____

Are you OK? What happened?

YOU _____

Could you still get here before eleven?

YOU _____

B. Personalization. Talk about a problem you had going to work or class.

Reading

RAPID Transit Schedule

State Street Line

Monday through Friday
Metro Airport to Downtown Station
E Express trains do <u>not</u> stop at Lake Park or Brown Avenue.

Metro Airport	Lake Park	North Mall	Brown Avenue	Downtown Station
6:26	6:33	6:42	6:53	7:09
E 6:53	X	7:06	X	7:27
7:06	7:12	7:22	7:33	7:50
E 7:17	X	7:30	X	7:51
7:27	7:34	7:43	7:54	8:11

⊝ **State Street Line**

A. **Look at the schedule. What are the stops on the State Street Line?** _____

_____

B. **Critical thinking. Now read about the workers. Answer the questions. Circle the letter.**

Hong

1. Jack Hong took the 7:12 from Lake Park. What time will he arrive at North Mall?

   a. 7:06   **b.** 7:22   **c.** 7:33

Kibit

2. Barbara Kibit is at Brown Avenue at 7:30. She needs to arrive at Downtown Station before 8:00. Which train should she take?

   a. the 7:22   **b.** the 7:33   **c.** the 7:54

Salinas

3. It is 6:30. David Salinas is at the Metro Airport station. He missed the 6:26. He needs to go to Brown Avenue. What is the next train he could take?

   a. the 6:26   **b.** the 7:06   **c.** the 6:53

Torres

4. Rita Torres lives near Lake Park. She needs to arrive at Downtown Station before 8:00. Which trains could she take?

   a. the 6:33 or 7:12   **b.** the 6:33 or 7:17   **c.** the 7:12 or 7:34

🎧 **A.** Listen. Where does the customer want to go? Circle the letter.

    a. Los Angeles   **b.** Rialto

Leaves Arrives

🎧 **B.** Mario, Laura, and Hans have to go to a computer training class in Rialto. They can't leave before 7:30 a.m. They have to arrive before 10:00 a.m.

Listen to the announcement again. Write the departure and arrival times of trains they could take.

C. Mario and Laura decide to take the first possible train. Read the e-mail message to their supervisor.

From:	Alioto, Laura	CC:	Tarnoff, Mario
To:	Salamanca, Marta		

Subject: Train schedule

Message:
Hi, Marta:
Mario and I will arrive on the 9:14 train. We'll take a taxi from the train station. We'll be there before 10:00.

See you soon!
Laura

Send / Delete / Address

Hans has to take a later train. Choose a train for Hans. Complete his e-mail message.

From:	Gottsman, Hans	CC:	Tarnoff, Mario; Alioto, Laura
To:	Salamanca, Marta		

Subject: Train schedule

Message:
Hi, Marta:

Hans

Send / Delete / Address

For extra practice, go to page 143.

▶ **Do it yourself!**   A plan-ahead project

Collaborative activity. Bring in a train or bus schedule. Choose a place. Make plans to go there. You have to return home before 5:30. Which trains or buses can you take?

A. **Vocabulary. Complete each sentence. Write the words on the line.**

1. I missed the _____. When is the next local?
   express / fare

2. I'd like a _____ ticket. I don't have enough money for a round trip.
   local / one-way

3. Please arrive _____ 4:00. The meeting starts at 4:00 sharp.
   after / before

B. **Vocabulary. Write the time in numbers.**

1. Half past eight ___8:30___

2. Ten to nine _____

3. Twenty after eight _____

4. A quarter after eight _____

C. **Conversation. Choose your response. Circle the letter.**

1. "You just missed it."

   a. That's too bad. When's the next one? **b.** Is it still here?

2. "You could still make the 6:37. But you should hurry."

   a. Great. Thanks.   **b.** Well, could I buy a ticket for the 7:42?

3. "Did the 6:37 express leave yet?"

   a. Yes. In ten minutes.   **b.** Yes. Ten minutes ago.

D. **Grammar and reading. Read the bus schedule. Then answer the questions.**

Express buses in blue print			
Bayville	**Walden**	**Beacon**	**Salem**
6:00	6:25	6:55	7:00
6:10	X	6:55	7:00
6:15	X	7:00	7:05
6:20	6:45	7:15	7:20
6:20	X	7:05	7:10

1. When does the first express bus leave Bayville? _____

2. Katerina Valenti wants to arrive in Salem before 7:15. Which bus should she take from Walden? _____

3. Ali Petak wants to arrive in Salem before 7:15. Which buses could he take from Bayville? _____

_____

64   Unit 5

> **Do it yourself!**

1. Point. Name things in the picture.

A taxi

2. Talk about the schedule and the times.

The express to Chester leaves at 7:05.

3. Create conversations for the people.

A: What's the fare to Chester?
B: Round trip or one way?

4. Say more about the picture. Use your <u>own</u> words. Say as much as you can.

Now I can
❑ ask about schedules.
❑ explain lateness.
❑ read bus and train schedules.
❑ buy tickets and pay fares.
❑ _____.

Your supplies and resources

> **Vocabulary**

Objectives
- ask for help
- offer help
- talk about inventory
- order supplies

Picture dictionary

🎧 **A.** Listen.

A bedroom	**A bathroom**		**A supply closet**	
① a desk	⑦ a towel	⑬ a bath mat	⑮ trash bags	㉑ cleansers
② a bed	⑧ a washcloth	⑭ a shower	⑯ paper towels	㉒ a sponge
③ a pillow	⑨ toilet paper		⑰ a vacuum cleaner	㉓ furniture polish
④ a sheet	⑩ a toilet		⑱ a mop	㉔ glass cleaner
⑤ a blanket	⑪ a bathtub		⑲ a bucket	
⑥ a pillowcase	⑫ a sink		⑳ rubber gloves	

Housework

㉕ empty the trash

㉖ change the sheets

㉗ make the bed

㉘ vacuum the carpet

㉙ do the laundry

🎧 **B.** Listen again and repeat.

🎧 **C.** Listen to the hotel housekeepers. Then listen again and match each picture with a conversation. Write the letter on the line.

Conversation 1 _____

Conversation 2 _____

Conversation 3 _____

a.   b.   c.

D. Complete each sentence. Write the words on the line.

1.   All the sheets are dirty. Let's _____ the laundry this afternoon.
     make / do

2.   Oh, no. We're out of trash bags, and I have to _____ the trash.
     change / empty

3.   I made the beds. Now I have to _____ the carpet.
     vacuum / do

4.   Please don't use a paper towel with that cleanser. Use a _____.
     pillowcase / sponge

5.   Don't use _____ on the desk; it's for the windows.
     glass cleaner / furniture polish

➤ **Do it yourself!**

A. Personalization. Complete the chart. Add two cleaning supplies.

B. Discussion. Talk about the products.

Product	Cleans	Room
glass cleaner	windows and mirrors	bathroom, bedroom, kitchen
1.		
2.		

I use Sparkle glass cleaner at home. It cleans windows and mirrors. I use it in the bathroom, the bedroom, and the kitchen.

Practical conversations

🎧 **A. Listen and read.**

A: Could you please get me some
   towels from the cart?

B: I'd be glad to. Anything else?

A: No. Thanks for the help.
   I appreciate it.

B: Anytime.

🎧 **B. Listen again and repeat.**

**C. Pair work. Ask for something from a
supply room or a cart. Use the
pictures or your <u>own</u> words.**

A: Could you please get
   me some _____ from
   the _____?

B: _____. Anything else?

A: No. Thanks for the help.
   I appreciate it.

B: _____.

towels   washcloths   sheets   pillowcases

🎧 **A. Listen and read.**

A: Would you like me to put away the
   supplies?

B: Oh, thanks for offering, but I can do
   that myself.

A: Well, please let me know if there's
   anything I can do.

B: Actually, you could get me a sponge.

A: Sure. No problem.

🎧 **B. Listen again and repeat.**

C. Pair work. **Offer to help. Use the words in the box or your <u>own</u> words.**

A: Would you like me to _____?
B: Oh, thanks for offering, but I can do that myself.
A: Well, please let me know if there's anything I can do.
B: Actually, you could get me _____.
A: _____.

empty the trash
change the sheets
clean the bathroom
vacuum the bedroom

Model 3   Get supplies. Express gratitude.

🎧 **A.** **Listen and read.**

A: I'm going to the supply room.
   I need trash bags.
B: Actually, I do too. Could you get
   me some when you're there?
A: Sure. I'll be right back.
B: Thanks a million.

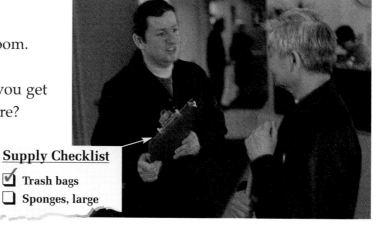

Supply Checklist
☑ Trash bags
☐ Sponges, large

🎧 **B.** **Listen again and repeat.**

C. Pair work. **Get supplies from a supply room or a cart.
Use the pictures or your <u>own</u> words.**

A: I'm going to the _____. I need _____.
B: Actually, I do too. Could you get me some
   when you're there?
A: _____. I'll be right back.
B: _____.

➤ Do it yourself!

Pair work. **Create a conversation
for the husband and wife.
What do they need?**

Practical grammar

Agreeing with too and either

affirmative	negative
He's vacuuming the carpet. I am **too**.	She's not working today. I'm not **either**.

A. Read each sentence. Then add a sentence. Use <u>too</u> or <u>either</u>.

1. We like clean bathrooms. (They) _____They do too._____

2. She has to work tomorrow. (We) _____

3. They need mops. (You) _____

4. He's emptying the trash. (I) _____

5. Tran doesn't see the cart. (I) _____I don't either._____

6. The plumbers aren't ready. (The electricians) _____

7. She's not making the bed. (He) _____

A / an and the

B. Look at the pictures. Write <u>a</u>, <u>an</u>, or <u>the</u> on the line.

1. I'm going to get ___an___ mop.

2. SUPPLIES — I'm going to get ___a___ mop.

3. Let's wash ___the___ window. It's very dirty.

4. I'm looking for ___an___ apartment.

The present continuous for the future

Use the present continuous to indicate what is happening right now.
> They**'re changing** the sheets now.

You can also use the present continuous to talk about the future.
> **A:** **Are** you **changing** the sheets tomorrow?
> **B:** No. We**'re changing** them tonight.

C. Answer the questions about <u>yourself</u>. Use the present continuous.

1. Are you cleaning the halls this afternoon?
   No, I'm cleaning them tomorrow morning.

2. Are you doing the laundry later?
   _____

3. What are you wearing to work tomorrow?
   _____

4. What are you doing next Wednesday night?
   _____

➤ Do it yourself!

Discussion. Talk about your plans for the weekend. Use the pictures or your <u>own</u> plans.

Next Sunday I'm washing the car.

Authentic practice 1

With words you know, YOU can talk to this co-worker.

A. Listen and read.

Co-worker: Hey, I'm so glad you're here.

YOU *Why? What's the problem?*

Co-worker: Well, the shift is starting in ten minutes, and we're out of practically everything! The guys last night didn't restock.

YOU *Is there anything I can do?*

Co-worker: Yes. Could you do me a big favor?

YOU *Sure.*

Co-worker: Would you be nice enough to get some supplies from the stockroom?

YOU *I'd be glad to. What do we need?*

Co-worker: A couple rolls of paper towels and some furniture polish . . . four or five containers of cleanser and a bunch of clean sponges.

YOU *Anything else?*

Co-worker: No. I think that's it for now. I don't like starting a shift without the right supplies.

YOU *I don't either. I'll be right back.*

B. Listen to the co-worker. Read your part out loud.

C. Listen and read. Choose your response. Circle the letter.

1. "Could you do me a big favor?"

   a. Is there anything I can do?   **b.** Sure.

2. "I'm out of practically everything!"

   a. I'm not either.   **b.** I am too.

3. "I think that's it for now."

   a. Do you need anything else?   **b.** Good.

D. Listen. Choose your response. Circle the letter.

1. **a.** Sure. No problem.   **b.** Thanks for offering.

2. **a.** Are you sure?   **b.** I don't either.

3. **a.** Thanks. I appreciate it.   **b.** OK. I'll be right back.

🎧 **A. Listen to the conversation. Then listen again. Write <u>yes</u> or <u>no</u>.**

1. Victor and Marie work at the same place. _____

2. Victor and Marie are ordering supplies. _____

🎧 **B. Listen again. Check ☑ Victor or Marie.**

	Victor	Marie
1. Who offers to help?	☐	☐
2. Who accepts help?	☐	☐
3. Who puts away the food?	☐	☐
4. Who puts the laundry in the laundry room?	☐	☐

🎧 **C. In your own words. Listen again. Answer the questions and then discuss your answers with a partner.**

1. What's the problem? _____

   _____

2. How do Victor and Marie solve the problem? _____

   _____

➤ Do it yourself!

A. Write your <u>own</u> response. Then read your conversation out loud with a partner.

I'm so busy today. Would you help me with something?

YOU _____

The supplies are coming in an hour. Could you open the stockroom for me?

YOU _____

I never have enough time!

YOU _____

B. Personalization. Talk about housework. Who does the housework in your house?

Authentic practice 2

Reading

A. **Read the supply checklist. Then answer the question.**

What are the supplies for? _____

The Wilton Towers

Supply Checklist

Stock the following for each room:

Item	Quantity	Item	Quantity	Item	Quantity
mini shampoo	1	face soap	1	bath mat	1
mini conditioner	1	washcloths	2	flat sheet	1
body lotion	1	bath towels	2	fitted sheet	1
bath soap	1	face towels	2	pillowcases	2

EVERY DAY Change bed linens and towels.
Replace personal care products. Empty trash.

B. **Critical thinking. Alex Palenko is a housekeeper on the third floor of the Wilton Towers Hotel. There are 10 guest rooms. Look at her supply cart. What supplies does she need?**

Palenko

1. __5__ shampoo
2. _____ conditioner
3. _____ body lotion
4. _____ bath soap

5. _____ face soap
6. _____ washcloths
7. _____ bath towels
8. _____ face towels

9. _____ bath mats
10. _____ flat sheets
11. _____ fitted sheets
12. _____ pillowcases

A. This is the supply room at Metropolitan Hospital. Look at the shelves and the inventory list. Does Ms. Cantu need to order supplies? Write <u>yes</u> or <u>no</u>. _____

Metropolitan Hospital
22 North Main, Mariposa Valley, TX 78294

Supply Room Inventory

Stock the following items at all times in these quantitites:

ITEM	QUANTITY
paper towels	6 cartons @ 24 rolls each
toilet paper	6 cartons @ 36 rolls each
cleanser, powdered	2 cartons @ 24 cans each
liquid soap	2 cartons @ 2 dozen each
glass cleaner, liquid	5 cartons @ 36 bottles each

B. Fill out the requisition form for the supplies Metropolitan Hospital needs.

Metropolitan Hospital
Central Supply Warehouse
22 North Main, Mariposa Valley, TX 78294

Requisition Form

Today's date: _____

Item	Quantity	Item	Quantity
paper towels	*5 cartons*		

For extra practice, go to page 144.

➤ Do it yourself!

A. Personalization. **What supplies are necessary in a new apartment? On a separate sheet of paper, make lists for the bathroom, the kitchen, and the bedroom.**

B. Discussion. **Compare lists. Do all the lists contain the same items?**

A. **Vocabulary. Where do you use these supplies? Write <u>bedroom</u> or <u>bathroom</u>.**

1. sheets _____
2. washcloths _____
3. blankets _____

4. bath mat _____
5. toilet paper _____
6. pillows _____

B. **Conversation. Choose <u>your</u> response. Circle the letter.**

1. "Would you like me to put away the blankets?"

   a. Thanks, but I can do that myself.　**b.** Please let me know if there's anything I can do.

2. "Could you please get me some cleanser?"

   a. I appreciate it.　　　　**b.** Sure. I'll be right back.

3. "Is there anything I can do to help?"

   a. Let me think.　　　　**b.** I'd be glad to.

C. **Grammar. Read each sentence. Then add a sentence. Use <u>too</u> or <u>either</u>.**

1. "I don't like these pillowcases."

   You: _____

2. "I'm not working tomorrow."

   You: _____

3. "I'm making the beds today."

   You: _____

D. **Writing. Complete each answer about <u>yourself</u>.**

1. Where are you going tomorrow? *Tomorrow* _____

   _____

2. What are you doing next Saturday? *Next Saturday* _____

   _____

➤ Do it yourself!

1. Point. Name things in the picture.
   Blankets

2. Ask questions about the picture.
   What's Rob doing on Monday?

3. Create conversations for the people.
   A: *Would you like me to put the laundry away?*
   B: *Yes. Thanks a million.*

4. Say more about the picture. Use your <u>own</u> words. Say as much as you can.

THIS WEEK
MONDAY — Rob – Work 8:30
TUESDAY
WEDNESDAY — Carla – Dentist 5:45

Now I can
❑ ask for help.
❑ offer help.
❑ talk about inventory.
❑ order supplies.
❑ _____.

Unit 6   77

Your relationships

► Vocabulary

Objectives
- express preferences
- talk about consequences
- understand procedures

Picture dictionary

🎧 **A. Listen.**

Work and community relationships

1. an employer
2. an employee
3. co-workers
4. partners
5. neighbors
6. a store owner
7. a landlord

Family relationships

8. relatives
9. grandparents
10. parents
11. children
12. a father-in-law
13. a daughter-in-law

Relating to others

14. discuss a problem
15. disagree
16. get along
17. break the rules
18. get hired
19. get fired
20. get a promotion

Other in-law relationships	Other words for "the boss"
a mother-in-law	employer
a son-in-law	supervisor
a sister-in-law	manager
a brother-in-law	owner

B. Listen again and repeat.

C. Listen to the conversations. Then listen again and choose a word or phrase for each conversation.

discuss a problem	break the rules	get a promotion	disagree

Conversation 1 _____

Conversation 2 _____

Conversation 3 _____

Conversation 4 _____

D. Complete each sentence. Write the words on the line.

1. All my _____ came to dinner last night—my parents, my
   <u>neighbors / relatives</u>
   grandparents, and all my sisters and brothers. It was great!

2. The new supervisor started today. He _____ yesterday morning.
   <u>got fired / got hired</u>

3. Jan doesn't _____ with her in-laws. They never agree on anything.
   <u>get along / disagree</u>

4. This is a big company. It has 200 _____.
   <u>employees / relatives</u>

➤ Do it yourself!

A. Personalization. List three people you have a relationship with.

At work	In my family	In my community
Carlos, my boss	Miriam, my daughter-in-law	Fred Lee, my landlord

B. Pair work. Tell your partner about one of the people in your chart. Say as much as you can.

Fred Lee is my landlord. He lives down the street. He gets along with all his neighbors.

Practical conversations

A. Listen and read.

A: I have a question. What will happen if I make a personal call?

B: I'm not sure. But it's against the rules. You'd better not.

A: Really? Well, thanks for telling me.

B: Anytime.

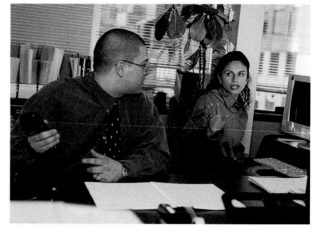

B. Listen again and repeat.

C. Pair work. Ask a partner about the rules. Use the pictures or your <u>own</u> words.

make a personal call

smoke in the building

park in the lot

A: I have a question. What will happen if I _____?

B: _____. But it's against the rules. You'd better not.

A: _____. Well, thanks for telling me.

B: _____.

A. Listen and read.

A: Would you rather work the day shift or the night shift?

B: That's a good question. I'd better check with my wife.

A: OK. But I need to know soon.

B: Can I tell you tomorrow?

A: Sure. Tomorrow's fine.

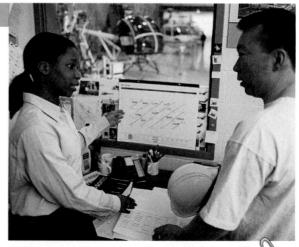

B. Listen again and repeat.

How to say it

the day shift / the night shift	the early shift / the late shift
the 7 a.m. shift / the 3 p.m. shift	the first shift / the second shift
from 9 to 5 / from 11 to 3	full-time / part-time

Pair work. Agree on a time.

    A: Would you rather work _____ or _____?
    B: _____. I'd better check with _____.
    A: _____. But I need to know soon.
    B: Can I tell you _____?
    A: Sure. _____'s fine.

Model 3   Discuss a problem. Offer and accept advice.

🎧 **A.** **Listen and read.**

    A: I just don't get along with my in-laws.
    B: I'm sorry to hear that. What's the problem?
    A: Well, we disagree about money.
    B: Maybe if you discuss it with them, you can work it out.
    A: I guess it's worth a try.

🎧 **B.** **Listen again and repeat.**

C. **Pair work. Discuss a disagreement. Use the topics in the box or talk about a <u>real</u> disagreement you have with someone.**

money	the children	the rent	the rules

    A: I just don't get along with my _____.
    B: I'm sorry to hear that. What's the problem?
    A: Well, we disagree about _____.
    B: Maybe if you discuss it with _____, you can work it out.
    A: I guess it's worth a try.

➤ Do it yourself!

Pair work. Create a conversation for the two men.

➤ Practical grammar

If in statements about the future

A. Complete the sentences with the simple present tense.

1. If the weather _____is_____ bad, we'll take the bus to work tomorrow.
   <small>be</small>

2. If Pedro and his partner _____ about money, they'll have to work it out.
   <small>disagree</small>

3. If she _____ the rules again, she won't get that promotion.
   <small>break</small>

4. If you _____ the laundry today, please tell your employer.
   <small>not do</small>

5. If he _____ with his mother-in-law, tell him to discuss the problem with her.
   <small>not get along</small>

6. What will happen if Silvio _____ in the wrong lot?
   <small>park</small>

7. Will you get a promotion if you _____ to work late every day?
   <small>go</small>

8. Fix the refrigerator if it _____.
   <small>not work</small>

B. Complete the sentences with your <u>own</u> words.

1. If you disagree with your in-laws, *discuss the problem with them.*

2. If you take the wrong train, _____

3. If it rains on Saturday, _____

Had better

It's going to rain. We'**d better take** our raincoats.

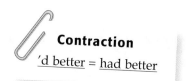

Contraction

'd better = had better

C. Complete each sentence with **'d better** or **had better** and your **own** words.

1. There's a lot of traffic. She _'d better leave early._

2. It's raining. They_____

3. Martin's supervisor called. Martin _____

4. Martha got fired. She_____

Would rather

Would you **rather vacuum** the offices or **clean** the kitchen floor?

I think I'**d rather vacuum** tonight.

D. Pair work. **Ask and answer these questions.**

1. Would you rather work in an office or at home?

2. Would you rather eat at home or in a restaurant tonight?

3. Would you rather do the laundry or cook dinner?

➤ Do it yourself!

A. Personalization. Complete the questionnaire about yourself.

B. Discussion. Work in a small group. Report your results to the rest of the class.

Two people in our group would rather work the night shift.

Preferences	yes	no	not sure
1. I'd rather work the night shift.	❑	❑	❑
2. I'd rather work part-time.	❑	❑	❑
3. I'd rather work in an office.	❑	❑	❑
4. I'd rather work with my family.	❑	❑	❑

Authentic practice 1

With words you know, YOU can talk to this store owner.

🎧 A. Listen and read.

Owner: Good morning, Mr. Tomic. What can I do for you today?

YOU *I have a question. Can you clean this jacket?*

Owner: Let me have a look. Oh, my goodness, what kind of stain is that?

YOU *Stain? Oh . . . it's tomato juice.*

Owner: To tell you the truth, I'm not sure if I can remove that. Maybe, maybe not. I can check. Can you wait a few minutes?

YOU *No. I'd better leave it. I have to go to work.*

Owner: OK. Well, if you call me from work, I'll tell you if I can get the stain out.

YOU *I'm sorry, but I can't make personal calls from work. I'd rather come here after 5:30. Is that OK?*

Owner: Sure, 5:30's fine. But I have to tell you that I might not be able to get it out.

YOU *Well, I like this jacket. It's worth a try.*

🎧 B. Listen to the store owner. Read your part out loud.

🎧 C. Listen and read. Choose your response. Circle the letter.

1. "What can I do for you today?"
   a. Today's fine.   **b.** I have a question. Can I leave this with you?

2. "Maybe I can do it, maybe not."
   a. I'd rather not.   **b.** Can you check?

3. "To tell you the truth, I won't be able to fix that."
   a. Thanks for telling me.   **b.** Can I tell you later?

🎧 D. Listen. Choose your response. Circle the letter.

1. **a.** Is 6:00 OK?   **b.** You'd better not.
2. **a.** It's against the rules.   **b.** I'd rather wait.
3. **a.** That's a good idea.   **b.** I'd rather check.

🎧 **A.** **Listen to the speaker. Then complete each sentence. Circle the letter.**

1. The woman speaking is _____.

   a. a new employee   **b.** a manager

2. The people listening are _____.

   a. new employees   **b.** sales managers

🎧 **B.** **Read the sentences. Then listen again and check ☑ yes, no, or I don't know.**

	yes	no	I don't know
1. New employees are supposed to get folders.	☐	☐	☐
2. Sales managers are supposed to be in the room across the hall.	☐	☐	☐
3. Employees with red folders are supposed to go to the cashier's office.	☐	☐	☐

🎧 **C.** **In your own words. Listen again. Answer the questions and then talk with a partner.**

1. What kind of meeting is this? _____

2. Who are the people? _____

3. What's the problem? _____

➤ Do it yourself!

A. **Write your own response. Then read your conversation out loud with a partner.**

Good morning.

YOU _____

What can I do for you today?

YOU _____

To tell you the truth, I'm not sure if I can do that. Can you wait a few minutes?

YOU _____

B. **Personalization. Tell your partner about a real conversation you had with a store owner in your neighborhood.**

Reading

A. Read the Brimstone Tire and Rubber Company employee manual.

BRIMSTONE
Tire and Rubber Company

Benefits for Families of Full-Time Employees

- *Emergency Childcare*
  If your regular childcare arrangements are disrupted and you need to find alternative childcare, Brimstone will provide up to two weeks' childcare at work for employees at the following Brimstone locations: Rubber City and Tulsa. Discuss with your personnel manager.

- *Family Illness or Injury Leave*
  If you have a child, spouse, or parent with a serious illness or injury, Brimstone will provide up to two weeks' time off with full pay to care for the relative or to find care for the relative. Discuss with your personnel manager.

- *Parental Leave (for new parents)*
  If a new child comes into an employee's home by birth, adoption, or foster care placement, Brimstone Tire will allow four weeks of paid parental leave. Additional leave without pay is also available in some situations. Discuss with your personnel manager.

General Rules and Requirements for Family Benefits

- If you know in advance that you will need emergency childcare or family illness or injury leave, please notify your personnel manager and fill out the necessary forms. Brimstone will do everything possible to serve your family in time of need.

- If you need parental leave, you MUST apply for it one month in advance. If you do not apply in advance, leave will automatically be without pay.

B. **Critical thinking. Read about these Brimstone full-time employees. What benefit can they get? Circle the letter.**

Barria

1. Marta Barria is a lathe operator in Tulsa. Her mother was in an accident. Marta needs a nurse's aide to care for her mother at home. She filled out a form the day after the accident. What benefit can Marta Barria get?

   a. parental leave   **b.** no benefit   **c.** family illness or injury leave

Roberts

2. Peter Roberts is a welder in Rubber City. On November 1, 2002, he and his wife adopted a baby girl from Korea. He told his personnel manager one month in advance. What benefit can he get?

   a. no benefit   **b.** parental leave   **c.** emergency childcare

Baraf

3. Yael Baraf works in the Belleville plant. She has four children. Usually Yael's sister-in-law takes care of them, but her sister-in-law is in the hospital and Yael has no childcare right now. She discussed the problem with her personnel manager and filled out a form. What benefit can she get?

   a. no benefit   **b.** emergency childcare   **c.** family illness or injury leave

Look at Yael Baraf's application for emergency childcare. Then complete an application for Peter Roberts.

BRIMSTONE
Tire and Rubber Company

Employee Benefits Application

Today's date: ___12___ ___2___ ___2002___
month   day   year

Employee name: ___Baraf___ ___Yael___
last name   first name

Employee work location: ___Belleville___

Check one: ☑ full-time   ☐ part-time

Benefit applied for (check one)
☑ Emergency Childcare
☐ Family Illness or Injury Leave
☐ Parental Leave

BRIMSTONE
Tire and Rubber Company

Employee Benefits Application

Today's date: _____
month   day   year

Employee name: _____
last name   first name

Employee work location: _____

Check one: ☐ full-time   ☐ part-time

Benefit applied for (check one)
☐ Emergency Childcare
☐ Family Illness or Injury Leave
☐ Parental Leave

For extra practice, go to page 145.

➤ Do it yourself!   A plan-ahead project

I get two weeks off with pay every year.

Discussion. Bring in employee manuals or benefits policies from your job or a relative's job. Or share an employee manual with a classmate. Discuss the policies.

A. Vocabulary. Complete the sentences with words from the box.

in-laws	landlord	disagree	partner	relatives	promotion

1. We don't get along. We _____ about everything.

2. Your grandmother and your father-in-law are your _____.

3. She got a _____, and now she's making more money.

4. I always send the rent check to my _____ by the tenth of the month.

B. Conversation. Choose <u>your</u> response. Circle the letter.

1. "What will happen if I break that rule?"
   a. I don't know.   **b.** I guess it's worth a try.

2. "I'd better check with my partner."
   a. That's fine.   **b.** I'll tell you tomorrow.

3. "Would you rather tell me tonight or tomorrow?"
   a. I'd better wait until tomorrow.   **b.** I need to know soon.

C. Grammar. Complete each sentence. Write the words on the line.

1. If you _____ the rules, will you get fired?
   break / will break

2. Please talk to the manager if you _____ parental leave.
   want / will want

3. If you _____ with your relatives, you'll have problems at home.
   won't get along / don't get along

D. Reading and writing. Read about Leonie Lipa. Then read the policy and complete the sentences.

Leonie Lipa works at Atlas Paper. She and her husband are adopting a child from Romania. They have to go there to pick up the baby, and they will have to stay for three weeks to complete the adoption process. Mrs. Lipa wants to take three weeks of parental leave to go to Romania.

> **Parental Leave Policy**
>
> All Atlas Paper employees are entitled to 6 weeks of paid parental leave. Normally, leave is taken immediately <u>after</u> the birth or adoption. If you'd rather take some or all of your parental leave <u>before</u> the birth or adoption, you must inform your manager one month in advance.

1. Mrs. Lipa would rather _____.

2. Mrs. Lipa had better _____.

➤ **Do it yourself!**

1. Point. Name people and things.
   Parents, a restaurant
2. Talk about the people.
   The relatives don't get along.
3. Create conversations for the people.
   A: Would you rather take the bus or the subway?
   B: Maybe I'd better take the bus.
4. Say more about the picture. Use your <u>own</u> words. Say as much as you can.

Now I can
❏ express preferences.
❏ talk about consequences.
❏ understand procedures.
❏ _____.

Your health and safety

> ## Vocabulary

Picture dictionary

Objectives
- understand and give warnings
- explain consequences of carelessness
- make suggestions and agree to them

🎧 **A. Listen.**

Safety and danger

1. a fire extinguisher
2. a smoke detector
3. a fire alarm
4. warning signs
5. slip
6. fall
7. jaywalk
8. get hit by a car
9. get hurt
10. get a shock
11. get burned
12. get sick
13. smell
14. hear
15. see

How often?

⑯ once a week   ⑰ twice a month   ⑱ three times a day

🎧 **B.** Listen again and repeat.

C. Answer the questions about <u>yourself</u>. Then compare your answers with a partner.

1. How many times a day do you drink water? _____

2. How many times a year do you go to the dentist? _____

3. How many times a week do you eat dinner at home? _____

🎧 **D.** Listen to the conversations. Then listen again and match each picture with a conversation. Write the letter on the line.

Conversation 1 _____   a.   b.   c.

Conversation 2 _____

Conversation 3 _____

➤ Do it yourself!

Look at the warning signs. Then complete the sentences with words from the box.

| get a shock | ~~get hit by a car~~ | get sick | get burned |

1. Watch out! You might *get hit by a car* .

2. Watch out! You might _____.

3. Watch out! You might _____.

4. Watch out! You might _____.

Practical conversations

Model 1   Warn someone about a danger.

A. Listen and read.

> **A:** Watch out!
> **B:** Why? What's wrong?
> **A:** That's dangerous. You might get a shock.
> **B:** You're right. Thanks for warning me.
> **A:** You're welcome.

B. Listen again and repeat.

C. Pair work. Warn your partner. Use the warning signs.

Warnings
Watch out!
Look out!
Be careful!

get a shock   get burned   slip   get hurt

> **A:** _____!
> **B:** Why? What's wrong?
> **A:** That's dangerous. You might _____.
> **B:** You're right. Thanks for warning me.
> **A:** _____.

Model 2   Report a dangerous situation and suggest action.

A. Listen and read.

> **A:** Uh-oh. I hear water.
> **B:** You'd better check the kitchen.
>   I'll check the supply room.
> **A:** Good idea. I'll be right back.
> **B:** Me too.

B. Listen again and repeat.

C. Pair work. **Express concern. Make a suggestion. Use the pictures and rooms from your home or workplace.**

    A: Uh-oh. I _____.
    B: You'd better check the _____.
          I'll check the _____.
    A: _____. I'll be right back.
    B: Me too.

Model 3   Remind someone to do something.

🎧 **A.** **Listen and read.**

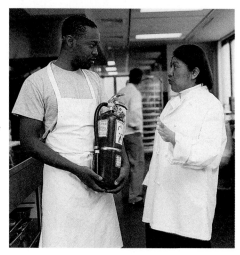

    A: How often should I test the fire extinguisher?
    B: Once a year. It's important. Don't forget.
    A: I won't. ╂
           won't
    B: And remember to test the smoke detector too.
    A: Don't worry. I will.

🎧 **B.** **Listen again and repeat.**

C. Pair work. **Remind someone to do something. Use the words in the box and real times.**

the batteries   the fire alarm   the smoke detector   the fire extinguisher

    A: How often should I test _____?
    B: _____ a _____. It's important. Don't forget.
    A: I won't.
    B: And remember to test _____ too.
    A: _____. I will.

➤ Do it yourself!

Pair work. **Look at the safety problems in the room. Create a conversation for the two people. Give warnings and suggest action.**

Practical grammar

Might

Don't go near the stove. You **might** get burned.

A. Look at the pictures. Then complete the warnings. Use <u>might</u> and the words in the box.

get sick	slip	get hit by a car	~~get a shock~~	get burned

1. Don't touch that! You _might get a shock_____.

2. Don't jaywalk! You _____.

3. Don't eat that! You _____.

4. Don't put your hand on the engine! You _____

   _____.

5. Don't walk on that wet floor! You _____.

Responding with <u>I will</u> and <u>I won't</u>

> Test the fire extinguisher once a year.

> OK. I will.

> Please don't leave the lights on when you go home.

> Don't worry. I won't.

B. **Complete each conversation with <u>I will</u> or <u>I won't</u>.**

1. **A:** Please tell me if you smell smoke.

   B: Don't worry. _____.

2. **A:** Don't touch that plug. You'll get a shock.

   B: _____.

3. **A:** Talk to your manager tomorrow.

   B: OK. _____.

4. **A:** If you get hurt, call the medical department.

   B: No problem. _____.

5. **A:** Please remember to check for gas.

   B: All right. _____.

6. **A:** Don't forget to replace the battery.

   B: _____.

➤ Do it yourself!

Pair work. Choose a warning sign.
Tell your partner what might happen.

> You might get burned! Be careful!

> I will. Thanks for warning me.

Unit 8   95

Authentic practice 1

With words you know, YOU can talk to this foreman.

⌒ A. Listen and read.

Foreman: There are a couple of important things I need to tell you. Mostly about safety. Why don't we meet in about ten minutes?

YOU: *Excuse me?*

Foreman: Let's talk in about ten minutes.

YOU: *OK. That's fine.*

[10 minutes later]

Foreman: OK. Two things here you've got to watch out for: fire and spills.

YOU: *Fire? No problem. Where are the fire extinguishers?*

Foreman: To the left of all the exit doors. Remember that.

YOU: *I will. But I don't understand—what are spills?*

Foreman: Spills? See this wet stuff on the floor? That's a spill. It's slippery. If you see a spill, be sure to put up a warning sign and call maintenance.

YOU: *Well, thanks for warning me. I won't forget.*

⌒ B. Listen to the foreman. Read your part out loud.

⌒ C. Listen and read. Choose your response. Circle the letter.

1. "There are a couple of things I'd better tell you about."

   a. Sure. I'll be right back.　　　　**b.** It's important.

2. "Why don't we check the smoke detectors?"

   a. I don't know.　　　　**b.** Good idea.

3. "See that stuff over there? Don't touch it."

   a. I will. Thanks for warning me.　　　　**b.** I won't. Thanks for warning me.

🎧 **D.** Listen. Choose <u>your</u> response. Circle the letter.

1. **a.** I will.   **b.** I won't.
2. **a.** What's wrong?   **b.** Thanks for warning me.
3. **a.** Don't worry. I will. **b.** Don't worry. I won't.

Listening comprehension

🎧 **A.** Listen to the announcement. Then answer the questions. Circle the letter.

1. What is the speaker talking about?
    a. smoke detectors   **b.** fire extinguishers

2. According to the speaker, what might save your life?
    a. smelling smoke   **b.** hearing the beep-beep sound

🎧 **B.** Listen again. What should you remember about smoke detectors?

_____

C. In your own words. Answer the questions about smoke detectors and then discuss your answers with a partner.

1. Where are the smoke detectors where you live or work? _____

    _____

2. Why are smoke detectors important? _____

    _____

➤ Do it yourself!

A. Write your <u>own</u> response. Then read your conversation out loud with a partner.

> Welcome. It's nice to have you at the plant.

YOU _____

> Why don't we schedule some time to talk about safety?

YOU _____

> But in the meantime, don't go near that stuff over there.

YOU _____

B. Personalization. Talk about fire extinguishers at home and at work. Where are they? Why are they important?

Reading

A. Read the fire safety warnings.

What to do in case of fire:
- If the fire is small, use the fire extinguisher.
- If the fire is large, leave the building fast. Use the nearest exit.
- Use the stairs. Don't use the elevator.
- Call 911. Report the fire.
- Don't go back into a burning building.

When NOT to fight a fire:
- If the fire is spreading too fast
- If the fire is too large
- If the fire might block your only exit
- If you don't know how to use the fire extinguisher

If any of the above conditions exist, leave the building immediately!

B. Critical thinking. Read about these situations. Then choose advice for each person. Circle the letter.

Cueva

1. Julio Cueva is on the tenth floor, cooking dinner for his children. There's a small fire in his kitchen. He has a fire extinguisher. He knows how to use it.

   a. Use the fire extinguisher.   b. Take the elevator to the first floor and call 911.

   Explain your answer: _If the fire is small, use the fire extinguisher._

Shufang

2. Li Shufang is working in a garage. There's a small fire in front of the exit door. She has a fire extinguisher, and she knows how to use it.

   a. Use the fire extinguisher.   b. Leave the building fast and call 911.

   Explain your answer: _____

Lulov

3. Marek Lulov discovers a small fire on the second floor at work. He has a fire extinguisher but isn't sure how to use it.

   a. Leave immediately. Go down the stairs. Call 911.   b. Call 911. Then use the fire extinguisher.

   Explain your answer: _____

A. On Saturday, Julio Cueva has a training session at work. His sister Paula is going to take care of his children. Read Julio's note to Paula.

Dear Paula:

Thanks a million for babysitting the kids. I'll be back around 6:30. If Maria has a fever, please call Dr. Lopez. Her number is 565-7222. If Eduardo wants to go to the soccer game, he'll tell you. It's OK. He can go with his friend.

Be careful when you do the laundry. The floor is always wet in the laundry room, and you might slip.

See you later. And thanks again!

Love,

Julio

B. Write a note to someone who is helping you with something. Thank the person and warn him or her about a possible problem. Use Julio's note as a model.

For extra practice, go to page 146.

➤ Do it yourself!   A plan-ahead project

Discussion. Find a fire extinguisher at home, at school, or at work. Read the directions. Or read the directions on this fire extinguisher. Talk about the directions with your classmates.

INSTRUCTIONS		
1. HOLD UPRIGHT. PULL RING PIN.	2. STAND BACK 10 FEET. AIM AT BASE OF FLAME.	3. SQUEEZE LEVER. SWEEP SIDE TO SIDE.

A. Vocabulary. Complete each sentence. Write the words on the line.

1. Don't touch that. You might _____.
   fall / get burned

2. Don't jaywalk. You might _____.
   get a shock / get hit by a car

3. Don't walk on that wet floor. You might _____.
   get sick / slip

B. Conversation. Choose <u>your</u> response. Circle the letter.

1. "Don't forget. It's important."

   a. I will.   **b.** I won't.

2. "Remember to check the smoke detector."

   a. OK.   **b.** Me too.

3. "I'll be right back."

   a. OK. See you soon.   **b.** Uh-oh.

4. "Why don't you check the hall?"

   a. I don't know.   **b.** Good idea.

C. Grammar. Complete each response with <u>I will</u> or <u>I won't</u>.

1. "Remember to check the battery." OK, _____.

2. "Don't forget to install a smoke alarm on each floor." OK, _____.

3. "Please get a new fire extinguisher from the supply room." OK, _____.

4. "If you smell gas, call 911." OK, _____.

D. Reading and writing. Look at the signs. Write your <u>own</u> warning. Use <u>might</u>.

1. *Be careful. You might get sick.* _____

2. _____

3. _____

➤ Do it yourself!

1. Point. Talk about the people and things.

   He's cleaning the hall. There's a warning sign in the hall.

2. Ask questions about the picture.

   Where's the fire extinguisher?

3. Create conversations for the people.

   A: Uh-oh.
   B: What's wrong?

4. Say more about the picture. Use your <u>own</u> words. Say as much as you can.

Now I can
- ❑ understand and give warnings.
- ❑ explain consequences of carelessness.
- ❑ make suggestions and agree to them.
- ❑ _____.

STAIRS

WET FLOOR

FIRE ALARM

Your money

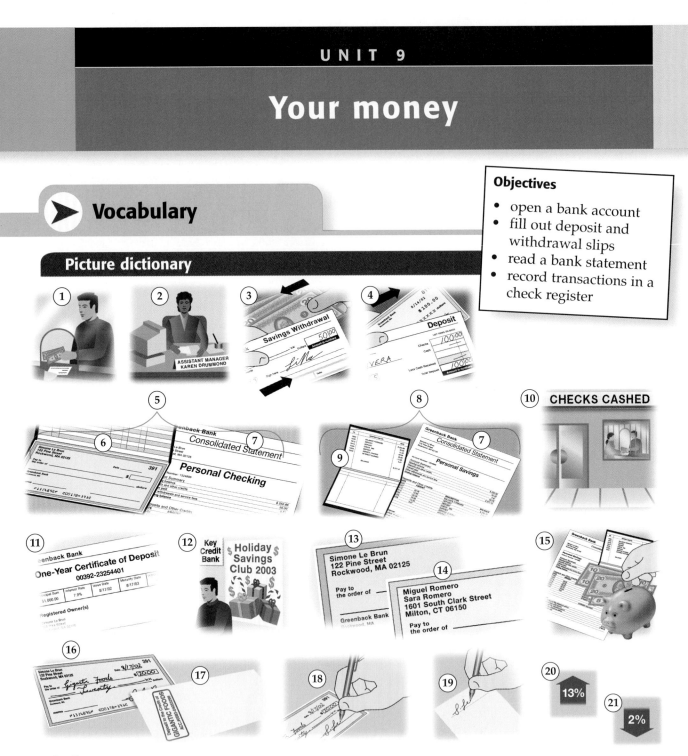

➤ Vocabulary

Picture dictionary

🎧 **A.** Listen.

Banking

1. a bank teller
2. a bank officer
3. a withdrawal
4. a deposit
5. a checking account
6. a checkbook
7. a statement

8. a savings account
9. a passbook
10. a check-cashing office
11. a certificate of deposit (a CD)
12. a holiday savings club
13. an individual account
14. a joint account

15. save
16. the front
17. the back
18. sign
19. endorse
20. high
21. low

102   Unit 9

Bank Statements

Account Summary	
Balance carried forward	$250.66
Monthly fee	$10.00 –
BALANCE	$240.66

Account Summary	
Balance carried forward	$300.53
Interest rate 3.5 %	
Interest earned	$10.52 +
BALANCE	$311.05

(22) a fee

(23) interest

B. Listen again and repeat.

C. Listen to the conversations. Then listen again and complete each sentence. Use words from the box.

> ATM fees   endorsing a check   a holiday savings club

Conversation 1 They're talking about _____.

Conversation 2 They're talking about _____.

Conversation 3 They're talking about _____.

D. Complete each sentence. Write the words on the line.

1. You can't deposit this check if you don't endorse the _____ and write your account number on it.
   front / back

2. I want a savings account with a _____ interest rate.
   high / low

3. I'd like a bank where the fees are _____.
   high / low

4. My husband and I would like to open _____ checking account.
   an individual / a joint

5. I think I was overcharged on my checking fees. Please look at my _____.
   statement / checkbook

➤ Do it yourself!

A. Personalization. Where do you save money? Where do your classmates save money? Complete the chart. Use these words or your own words.

> a savings account
> a holiday savings club
> a certificate of deposit (a CD)

Name	Where?
Alex	in a CD

B. Collaborative activity. Where else do your classmates save money? Make a list and then discuss it.

Andre saves money in an IRA.

Practical conversations

A. Listen and read.

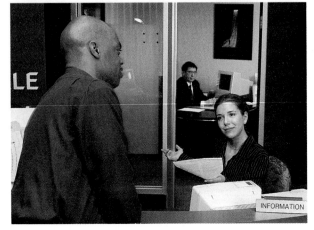

A: I'd like to open a checking account.

B: Certainly. Just fill out this form and take it to an officer.

A: Oh. By the way, which CD pays the highest interest?

B: I'm not positive. I'll check.

B. Listen again and repeat.

C. Pair work. **Use a bank. Ask for information. Use the ideas in the box.**

make a deposit ·················	deposit slip ················	a teller
make a withdrawal ·············	withdrawal slip ·········	a teller
apply for a credit card ········	form ····························	an officer
open an account ················	form ····························	an officer

A: I'd like to _____.

B: Certainly. Just fill out this _____ and take it to _____.

A: Oh. By the way, which _____ pays the highest interest?

B: I'm not positive. I'll check.

A. Listen and read.

A: I'm interested in getting an ATM card.

B: OK. Why don't you have a seat? I'll get you the forms.

A: By the way, how long will it take?

B: It won't take long. About a week.

B. Listen again and repeat.

C. Pair work. **Ask how long something will take. Use the ideas in the box.**

A: I'm interested in _____.

B: _____. Why don't you have a seat? I'll get you the forms.

A: By the way, how long will it take?

B: It won't take long. About _____.

> opening a checking account
> applying for a credit card
> buying a CD

Model 3 Cash a check. Remember something you forgot to do.

A. Listen and read.

A: Excuse me. I'd like to cash this paycheck.

B: Sure. I'll be right with you.

A: Oops. I forgot to endorse the back. Just a second.

B: OK. How would you like that?

A: Let me think. . . . Twenties, tens, and singles, please.

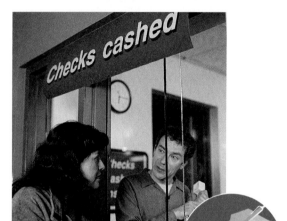

B. Listen again and repeat.

C. Pair work. **Cash a paycheck or a personal check. Remember something you forgot to do. Use the ideas in the box and your <u>own</u> words.**

A: Excuse me. I'd like to cash this _____.

B: _____. I'll be right with you.

A: Oops. I forgot to _____. Just a _____.

B: _____. How would you like that?

A: Let me think. . . . _____, please.

> endorse the back
> fill out a deposit slip
> write my account number on the back

➤ Do it yourself!

A. Personalization. **Complete the information on the paycheck and fill out the deposit slip. Use your <u>own</u> name and address.**

B. Pair work. **Create a conversation between a customer and a bank officer or teller. Use the check and deposit slip in your conversation.**

I'd like to deposit this check.

Statement Of Earnings ▼ Detach at perforation and keep for your records. ▼

FLUSHING PLUMBING SUPPLY   County Bank
17 Park Street   Monrovia, CA 91016
Monrovia, CA 91016
                                  A1354
                                  DATE: 05/11/02
PAY   SIX HUNDRED AND 25/100 . . . . DOLLARS
                                  $*****600.25
TO THE
ORDER OF _____

_____   *Carinne J Myyu*

THE BACK OF THIS DOCUMENT CONTAINS AN ARTIFICIAL WATERMARK-HOLD AT AN ANGLE TO VIEW
⑆050364⑆ ⑈071923284⑈: 79⑊061021⑆

⊙ STATEMENT SAVINGS DEPOSIT

KC   KEY CREDIT BANK   DATE _____

ACCOUNT NUMBER   CASH ▶
[ ][ ][ ][ ][ ][ ][ ]   CHECKS ▶

                              ENDORSE ALL
                              CHECKS
                              ___
                              NOTIFY TELLER OF
                              ANY CHANGE OF
                              ADDRESS

NAME _____   TOTAL $

Practical grammar

Comparisons with adjectives: superlatives

Which bank pays **higher** interest, the State Bank or the City Bank?

State Bank
3.5%
interest on
savings

City Bank
3.8%
interest on
savings

County Bank
3.9%
interest on
savings

Bonds
tumble

The City Bank. But the County Bank pays **the highest** interest in town.

Use comparatives to compare two people, places, or things.
Use superlatives to compare more than two people, places, or things.

adjective	comparative form	superlative form
high	higher	the highest
important	more important	the most important
good	better	the best
bad	worse	the worst

A. **Complete each sentence with the superlative form of the adjective.**

1. The check-cashing office on First Street is busier than the one on Main. But the one on Third Street is _the busiest_.
   busy

2. The fees at National First Bank are lower than the fees at Green Bank. The fees at Key Credit Bank are _____.
   low

3. You're getting 9% interest on a 3-month CD? That's _____ interest in the country.
   high

4. What's _____ savings bank in the city?
   good

5. What's _____ thing to ask about a holiday savings club?
   important

6. I don't like to drive on the old road. It's _____ road in the state.
   dangerous

7. This is _____ restaurant in town; it's dirty and the service is bad.
   bad

Questions of degree

How **long** will it take to get an ATM card?

Not long. About ten business days.

How long were you at the bank? — For an hour.
How soon can you send me the checks? — In about ten days.
How high is the interest rate on a passbook savings account? — It's 3%, I think. But I'm not positive.

B. Complete each question with **How** and words from the box.

~~good~~	busy	far	late	important	high	cold

1. _____How good_____ is the customer service at the Mutual Bank?

2. _____ is the winter here?

3. _____ is the check-cashing office open?

4. _____ is a high interest rate when you choose a bank?

5. _____ are the ATM fees here?

6. _____ is the bank at lunch time?

7. _____ is your bank from your workplace?

➤ Do it yourself!

A. Personalization. What's _your_ opinion? Fill out the survey about _your_ city or town.

The best bank	
The best restaurant	
The best hospital	
The best clothing store	
The best supermarket	

B. Discussion. Compare opinions with your classmates.

Eduardo's has the best food.

Maybe. But how good is the service there?

With words you know, YOU can talk to this bank officer.

A. Listen and read.

Officer: Good morning. What can we do for you today?

YOU *I'd like to open an account.*

Officer: Fine. What kind of account were you thinking of?

YOU *A checking account.*

Officer: Joint or individual?

YOU *Joint, please. For me and my wife.*

Officer: OK. Why don't you just step this way and have a seat? I'll be right with you.

YOU *By the way, I'm interested in getting an ATM card too.*

Officer: Certainly. I'll get you a form to fill out for your PIN.

YOU *PIN?*

Officer: Personal Identification Number. You'll need one for the ATM. Make yourself comfortable. I'll only be a minute.

B. Listen to the bank officer. Read your part out loud.

C. Listen and read. Choose your response. Circle the letter.

1. "What can we do for you today?"
   a. You can have a seat.   **b.** I'm interested in opening an account.

2. "Please step this way. I'll be right with you."
   a. OK. Thank you.   **b.** I'm not positive.

3. "Why don't you have a seat?"
   a. Thanks. I will.   **b.** Because I already have one.

D. Listen. Choose your response. Circle the letter.

1. **a.** Joint or individual?   **b.** Oops, I forgot to endorse it. Just a second.

2. **a.** OK. Thanks.   **b.** Yes, please.

3. **a.** Fives and tens, thanks.   **b.** It won't take long.

🎧 **A.** Listen to the automated customer service line from the State Bank. Then read the Customer Services chart.

Customer Services

☐ Verify account balances   ☐ Talk to a financial adviser

☐ Open a checking account   ☐ Open a savings account

☐ Transfer money into another account   ☐ Apply for an ATM card

☐ Pay bills   ☐ Change a PIN number

🎧 **B.** Listen again. Check ☑ the <u>four</u> things you can do by telephone.

🎧 **C.** Listen again. Then answer the questions <u>yes</u>, <u>no</u>, or <u>I don't know</u>.

1. Does the caller have an account with the State Bank? _____

2. How many languages does the caller speak? _____

D. In your own words. Discuss these bank services: ATMs, automated customer service lines, talking to bank officers and tellers.
Which is the best? Which is the easiest? Which is the worst?

ATMs are the easiest.

➤ Do it yourself!

A. Write your <u>own</u> response. Then read your conversation out loud with a partner.

Good afternoon. What can we do for you?

YOU _____

Certainly. Please have a seat at my desk.

YOU _____

I'll be right with you. I just have to get some forms.

YOU _____

B. Personalization. In your opinion, what's a good bank? What's a bad bank?

Reading

A. Look at the bank statement. Then check ☑ the information the statement has.

Greenback Bank – Statement

Name: Liliana Ortiz
63 Maple Street
Los Pinos, AZ 85018

Statement period: January 22–February 20, 2002
Automated Customer Service: 800-555-7232

Primary Account Number: 507-3327
Number of checks enclosed: 2

Summary of Accounts

TYPE		OPENING BALANCE	CLOSING BALANCE
Checking	507-3327	$ 823.55	$1197.89
Savings	507-3328	$2300.36	$2302.55
Holiday Club	507-2002	$ 50.00	$ 75.00
CD-6-month	507-0001	$ 500.00	$ 500.00

Activity — Basic Checking

1/22	Opening balance	$823.55
1/22	ATM withdrawal	$100.00
1/22	ATM fee	$ .75
1/28	Customer check #110	$450.00
1/29	Customer check #111	$ 12.00
2/8	Deposit	$935.52 +
2/19	Interest credit	$ 1.57 +

1. ☐ the customer's name

2. ☐ the customer's phone number

3. ☐ the interest rate for the 6-month CD

4. ☐ the statement period

5. ☐ the balance in the checking account

6. ☐ the bank's address

7. ☐ the customer service phone number

8. ☐ the deposits and withdrawals

B. Critical thinking. **Look at these bank documents and the bank statement in Exercise A. Then answer the questions.**

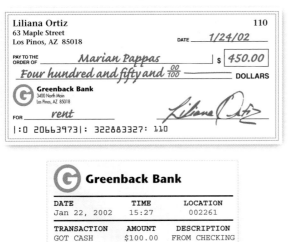

Liliana Ortiz
63 Maple Street
Los Pinos, AZ 85018

110

DATE _1/24/02_

PAY TO THE
ORDER OF _Marian Pappas_ | $ 450.00

Four hundred and fifty and 00/100 — DOLLARS

Greenback Bank
3400 North Main
Los Pinos, AZ 85018

FOR _rent_

|:0 20663973|: 322883327: 110

Liliana Ortiz
63 Maple Street
Los Pinos, AZ 85018

111

DATE _1/26/02_

PAY TO THE
ORDER OF _Discount Drugs_ | $ 12.00

twelve and 00/100 — DOLLARS

Greenback Bank
3400 North Main
Los Pinos, AZ 85018

FOR

|:0 20663973|: 322883327: 111

Greenback Bank

DATE	TIME	LOCATION
Jan 22, 2002	15:27	002261

TRANSACTION	AMOUNT	DESCRIPTION
GOT CASH	$100.00	FROM CHECKING
ATM FEE	$ .75	
BALANCE		
Available now	$722.80	

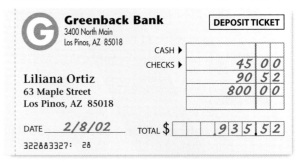

Greenback Bank
3400 North Main
Los Pinos, AZ 85018

DEPOSIT TICKET

	CASH ▶			
	CHECKS ▶	45	0	0
		90	5	2
		800	0	0

Liliana Ortiz
63 Maple Street
Los Pinos, AZ 85018

DATE _2/8/02_   TOTAL $ | 9 | 3 | 5 | 5 | 2 |

322883327: 28

1. When did Ms. Ortiz make a deposit? _____

2. When did she get cash from the ATM? _____

3. When did she write the check to Marian Pappas? _____

4. How long did it take for the bank to receive the check Ms. Ortiz wrote to Discount Drugs? _____

Writing

A. Look at the entries in Liliana Ortiz's check register. Then answer the questions.

Ortiz

ITEM NO. OR TRANS. CODE	DATE	TRANSACTION DESCRIPTION	SUBTRACTIONS AMOUNT OF PAYMENT OR WITHDRAWAL (-)	(-) FEE IF ANY	ADDITIONS AMOUNT OF DEPOSIT OR PAYMENT(+)	BALANCE
						823 55
	1/22	ATM withdrawal	100 00	.75		100 75
						722 80
110	1/24	Marian Pappas rent	450 00			450 00
						272 80
111	1/26	Discount Drugs	12 00			12 00
						260 80
	2/8	Deposit			935 52	935 52
						1196 32
	2/19	Interest			1 57	1 57
						1197 89

1. How much money did Ms. Ortiz withdraw from the ATM? _____

2. What was the fee? _____

B. Enter the transactions for the activity on February 22, 23, and 25. Use the check register in Exercise A.

DATE	TIME	LOCATION
Feb 22, 2002	8:14	002249

TRANSACTION	AMOUNT	DESCRIPTION
GOT CASH	$80.00	FROM CHECKING
ATM FEE	$ .75	

Greenback Bank
3400 North Main
Los Pinos, AZ 85018

DEPOSIT TICKET

CASH ▶
CHECKS ▶ 800 00

Liliana Ortiz
63 Maple Street
Los Pinos, AZ 85018

DATE 2/23/02   TOTAL $ 800.00

322883327: 28

Liliana Ortiz   112
63 Maple Street
Los Pinos, AZ 85018   DATE 2/25/02

PAY TO THE ORDER OF   Dr. Stanley Arzoomanian $ 45.00

Forty-five ————————————— DOLLARS

Greenback Bank
3400 North Main
Los Pinos, AZ 85018

FOR _____

|:0 20663973|: 322883327: 112

For extra practice, go to page 147.

▶ Do it yourself!   A plan-ahead project

Discussion. Collect bank documents such as withdrawal slips, deposit slips, and deposit envelopes from your bank. Then compare them with the ones your classmates found.

• How are they the same?

• How are they different?

• Which ones are the easiest to use?

Review

A. Vocabulary. Complete each sentence. Write the words on the line.

1. What's the interest rate on a one-year _____?
   passbook / CD

2. I'm leaving the Greenback Savings Bank. The fees are too _____.
   high / low

3. You'd better _____ the back of the check if you want to deposit it.
   endorse / save

B. Conversation. Choose your response. Circle the letter.

1. "How would you like that?"
   a. In fives and tens.   b. I'd like to cash this check.

2. "Just a minute. I'll be right with you."
   a. Great.   b. You're right.

3. "I'll check."
   a. Where do I endorse it?   b. Thanks. How long will it take?

C. Grammar. Complete each sentence. Write an adjective on the line.

1. How _____ are the fees at Mid-State Bank?
   high / higher

2. Which bank has the _____ customer service in town?
   better / best

3. How _____ is good service?
   important / most important

4. That check-cashing office has the _____ check-cashing fees in this city.
   worse / worst

D. Reading and writing. Look at the check and the deposit slip. Record the transactions in the check register.

Li Na
5 North Way
Lake Lara, FL 33126   101
DATE 8/17/02
PAY TO THE ORDER OF Best Foods $ 18.45
Eighteen and 45/100 _____ DOLLARS
Florida FEDERAL BANK
75 Grace Street, Lake Lara, FL 33126
Li Na
|:0 26063739|: 38822338|: 101

Li Na
5 North Way
Lake Lara, FL 33126   DEPOSIT TICKET
CASH ▶
CHECKS ▶   120 78
DATE 8/19/02
Florida FEDERAL BANK
75 Grace Street, Lake Lara, FL 33126
TOTAL $ 120 78
38822338|: 22

ITEM NO. OR TRANS. CODE	DATE	TRANSACTION DESCRIPTION	SUBTRACTIONS AMOUNT OF PAYMENT OR WITHDRAWAL (-)	(-) FEE IF ANY	ADDITIONS AMOUNT OF DEPOSIT OR PAYMENT(+)	BALANCE
						457 22

112   Unit 9

GREENBACK BANK

➤ Do it yourself!

1. **Point. Name people and things.**
   A teller, an ATM

2. **Ask questions about the picture.**
   Which account pays the highest interest?

3. **Create conversations for the people.**
   A: How would you like that?
   B: Twenties and tens, please.

4. **Say more about the picture. Use your <u>own</u> words. Say as much as you can.**

Interest rates:

Checking with interest 1%.
Passbook savings 1.5%
Statement savings 1.8%

Certificates of deposit

6 month   4.5%
1 year   5%
2 year   5.8%

SEPTEMBER 4

ATM
Get cash
See information
Transfer funds
Make deposits

ATM FEES

INFORMATION

CHECKING ACCOUNT APPLICATION

Now I can
- ❑ open a bank account.
- ❑ fill out deposit and withdrawal slips.
- ❑ read a bank statement.
- ❑ record transactions in a check register.
- ❑ _____.

Your career

Vocabulary

Picture dictionary

Objectives
- understand company-paid benefits
- follow company policies
- understand paychecks and pay stubs

A. Listen.

Health insurance

1. a medical plan
2. claim forms
3. an insurance card
4. a co-payment
5. a dental plan
6. a vision plan
7. a reimbursement
8. sign up
9. a dependent
10. choose

Benefits and related words

11. a vacation
12. retirement
13. a pension
14. a salary

Employment

⑮ **employed**: has a job

⑯ **unemployed**: doesn't have a job

⑰ **self-employed**: doesn't have a boss

🎧 **B.** Listen again and repeat.

🎧 **C.** Listen to the conversations. Then listen again and complete each sentence. Use words from the box.

a dental plan   a reimbursement   a pension

Conversation 1 They're talking about _____.

Conversation 2 They're talking about _____.

Conversation 3 They're talking about _____.

D. Complete each sentence. Write the words on the line.

Mr. and Mrs. Diaz live in Miami. Mr. Diaz works at King's Dental Supply, and

Mrs. Diaz is _____. She has her own business—she sells clothes

1. unemployed / self-employed

from Santo Domingo. Their son Joe is _____ right now. He's looking

2. unemployed / self-employed

for a job.

King's Dental Supply has great _____ for employees and

3. health insurance / co-payments

their _____, so Mrs. Diaz and Joe are covered too. For the

4. dependents / reimbursements

_____ plan, all they have to do is _____ a doctor

5. medical / dental   6. choose / sign up

and pay a small _____ when they have an appointment.

7. co-payment / reimbursement

➤ Do it yourself!

A. What kinds of benefits do you and your classmates have? Complete the chart with numbers.

B. Discussion. Talk about other kinds of benefits you or your classmates have.

Benefit	Number of students who have this benefit
a medical plan	
a dental plan	
a vision plan	
a retirement pension	
other benefits	

Practical conversations

🎧 **A.** Listen and read.

> **A:** Have you signed up for the medical plan yet?
> **B:** Yes, I have.
> **A:** And have you chosen a doctor?
> **B:** No, I haven't. Not yet.
> **A:** Well, we're supposed to do that by 5:00 today.
> **B:** I know. Thanks for reminding me.

🎧 **B.** Listen again and repeat.

C. Pair work. **Ask about a benefits plan. Remind your partner about an obligation. Use the words in the box.**

medical plan	a doctor	dental plan	a dentist	vision plan	an optician

> **A:** Have you signed up for the _____ yet?
> **B:** Yes, I have.
> **A:** And have you chosen _____?
> **B:** No, I haven't. Not yet.
> **A:** Well, we're supposed to do that by _____.
> **B:** I know. Thanks for reminding me.

🎧 **A.** Listen and read.

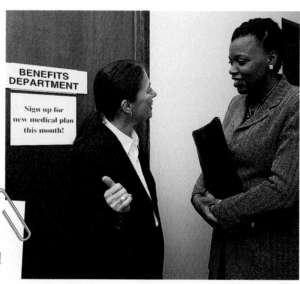

> **A:** Hey, Monica, guess what!
> **B:** What?
> **A:** We're going to get six more vacation days.
> **B:** No kidding. That's terrific. When does the new policy start?
> **A:** Immediately.

🎧 **B.** Listen again and repeat.

🎧 **Approval**
terrific
wonderful
fantastic

116   Unit 10

C. Pair work. **Break news about a vacation or sick day policy. Use the words in the box and your <u>own</u> words.**

A: Hey, _____, guess what!

B: What?

A: We're going to get _____.

B: No kidding. That's _____. When does the new policy start?

A: _____.

> four more sick days
> five more vacation days

Model 3   Meet an old friend. Discuss bad news. Make a suggestion.

🎧 **A.** **Listen and read.**

A: Hi, Jack. Long time, no see. How's it going?

B: Not great. I lost my job.

A: Oh, no. How long have you been unemployed?

B: Since March 13.

A: Why don't you ask about a job where I work? There are some openings right now. And we have very good benefits.

🎧 **B.** **Listen again and repeat.**

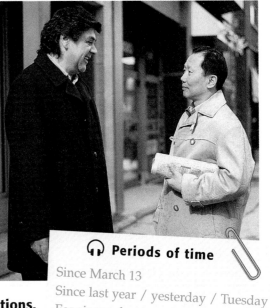

🎧 **Periods of time**

Since March 13
Since last year / yesterday / Tuesday
For six weeks

C. Pair work. **Talk about losing a job. Make suggestions. Use the benefits in the box and your <u>own</u> words.**

| vision plan | dental plan | sick leave policy |
| medical plan | vacation policy | |

A: Hi, _____. Long time, no see. How's it going?

B: _____. I lost my job.

A: Oh, no. How long have you been unemployed?

B: _____.

A: Why don't you ask about a job where I work?
There are some openings right now. And we have a terrific _____.

➤ **Do it yourself!**

Pair work. **Create a conversation for the people in the picture. Talk about benefits plans.**

Practical grammar

The present perfect with <u>already</u> and <u>yet</u>, <u>for</u> and <u>since</u>

<u>already</u> and <u>yet</u>

Have you **signed up** for the medical plan <u>yet</u>?

Yes, I <u>already</u> **have.**

Have you **chosen** a doctor?

No, I **haven't.** <u>Not yet</u>.

<u>for</u> and <u>since</u>

How long **have** you **been** here?

I've been here <u>for</u> about two years. What about you?

I've been here <u>since</u> August 2001.

Use <u>have</u> or <u>has</u> and a past participle for the present perfect. The past participle of regular verbs is like the simple past form (verb + -<u>ed</u>).

past participle

I **have worked** here for a year.

past participle

Maria **has lived** in Chicago since May.

🎧 **Past participles of irregular verbs**

Verb	Past participle		Verb	Past participle
be	been		read	read
choose	chosen		speak	spoken
do	done		take	taken

There is a complete list of past participles of irregular verbs on page 135.

A. Complete the present perfect form of each verb.

1. Have you _____*taken*_____ all your sick days yet?

take

2. How long has he _____ in that plan?

be

3. They have already _____ to their doctor about the co-payment.

speak

4. Haven't you _____ the claim form yet?

read

5. We've already _____ the plan, but it hasn't started yet.

choose

6. I haven't _____ that since last year.

do

7. We _____ at Rosa's Painting for five years.

work

8. How long _____ they _____ employed here?

be

9. She _____ her vacation days since 2001.

not take

118   Unit 10

Be supposed to and suggestions with Why

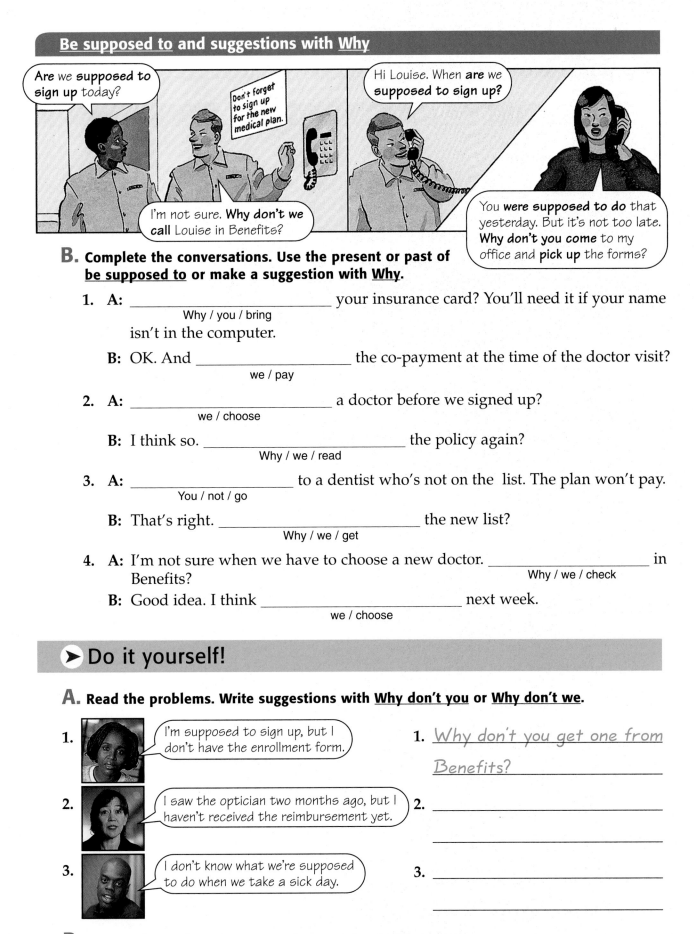

B. Complete the conversations. Use the present or past of be supposed to or make a suggestion with Why.

1. **A:** _____ your insurance card? You'll need it if your name
    <u>Why / you / bring</u>
    isn't in the computer.

    B: OK. And _____ the co-payment at the time of the doctor visit?
    <u>we / pay</u>

2. **A:** _____ a doctor before we signed up?
    <u>we / choose</u>

    B: I think so. _____ the policy again?
    <u>Why / we / read</u>

3. **A:** _____ to a dentist who's not on the list. The plan won't pay.
    <u>You / not / go</u>

    B: That's right. _____ the new list?
    <u>Why / we / get</u>

4. **A:** I'm not sure when we have to choose a new doctor. _____ in
    Benefits?   <u>Why / we / check</u>

    B: Good idea. I think _____ next week.
    <u>we / choose</u>

➤ Do it yourself!

A. Read the problems. Write suggestions with Why don't you or Why don't we.

1. I'm supposed to sign up, but I don't have the enrollment form.

    1. <u>Why don't you get one from</u>
        <u>Benefits?</u>

2. I saw the optician two months ago, but I haven't received the reimbursement yet.

    2. _____
        _____

3. I don't know what we're supposed to do when we take a sick day.

    3. _____
        _____

B. Pair work. Read your conversations out loud with a partner.

> **With words you know, YOU can talk to this former co-worker.**

🎧 **A.** Listen and read.

Eva: Hey, Elaine! I haven't seen you in ages. How're you doing?

YOU *Eva! I'm OK! What about you?*

Eva: Well, to tell you the truth, pretty bad. I lost my job.

YOU *Oh, no. You lost your job? I'm sorry.*

Eva: Yeah, well, they closed the office and everyone got laid off.

YOU *That's awful.*

Eva: Well, I still have my benefits. And I'm getting unemployment. But I'm looking for a new job.

YOU *Why don't you talk to Ann in Customer Service? There are some openings right now.*

Eva: Really?

YOU *Yeah. I'll call Ann tomorrow morning. She really liked you. You were a great cashier.*

Eva: Thanks a million. I'm supposed to go to the unemployment office at 9:00, and I'd better be on time. What if I come in at about 10:00?

YOU *That's great. See you then.*

🎧 **B.** Listen to Eva. Read <u>your</u> part out loud.

🎧 **C.** Listen and read. Choose <u>your</u> response. Circle the letter.

1. "I haven't seen you in ages."

   a. I know. Long time, no see.   **b.** That's good. What about you?

2. "To tell you the truth, our benefits are terrible."

   a. No kidding. That's too bad.   **b.** That's terrific.

3. "What if I call Ann?"

   a. That sounds fine.   **b.** Why don't you call Ann?

🎧 **D.** Listen. Choose <u>your</u> response. Circle the letter.

1. **a.** Not great.   **b.** I'm going to sign up.

2. **a.** How long have you been unemployed?   **b.** Really? I'm sorry!

3. **a.** Yes! Thanks for reminding me.   **b.** Guess what!

Listening comprehension

🎧 **A.** Listen to the conversation. Then listen again and check ✓ <u>old plan</u> or <u>new plan</u>.

	old plan	new plan
1. Employees can use this year's vacation days next year.	❏	❏
2. Employees can't use this year's vacation days next year.	❏	❏
3. Employees get four weeks of vacation after seven years.	❏	❏
4. Employees get four weeks of vacation after five years.	❏	❏
5. Employees have three sick days.	❏	❏
6. Employees have five sick days.	❏	❏

B. In your own words. Answer the questions. Then discuss your answers with a partner.

1. What do <u>you</u> think is a good vacation or sick day policy? _____

_____

2. Who takes more vacation and sick days—people who work for a company, or people who are self-employed? _____

➤ Do it yourself!

A. Write your <u>own</u> response. Then read your conversation out loud with a partner.

It's been ages since I've seen you. How's it going?   **YOU** _____

Really?   **YOU** _____

What if I call you tomorrow?   **YOU** _____

B. Personalization. Talk about how many vacation days and sick days <u>you've</u> used this year.

Reading

A. Read Katrin Havel's paycheck and pay stub. Then complete each sentence. Circle the letter.

```
Statement Of Earnings     ▼ Detach at perforation below and keep for your records ▼

  Edison                           Mutual Bank
  Lighting                         Crane, Washington
                                             98343
                                   Date: 06/15/02
                                   Check No: 2330051

PAY   FIVE HUNDRED NINETY AND 39/100 . . . . . . . . . . . . . . . DOLLARS
                                   $*****590.39
TO THE
ORDER OF    Katrin Havel

II·32029II· I·2431111I: 2330051II:
```

Havel

```
  Edison                                    DATE: 06/15/02
  Lighting                           CHECK NO: 2330051

KATRIN HAVEL            PAY PERIOD: 6/01/02 TO 6/15/02
```

HOURS AND EARNINGS		TAXES AND DEDUCTIONS	
GROSS PAY	$737.10	MEDICAL INSURANCE	$8.55
		DENTAL INSURANCE	$2.66
		FEDERAL TAX	$85.20
		STATE TAX	$50.30
NET PAY	$590.39	TOTAL DEDUCTIONS	$146.71

```
RATE       $10.53
HOURS       70.00
EARNINGS  $737.10   YEAR-TO-DATE    $8104.80
```

PRE-TAX ITEMS	AFTER-TAX DEDUCTIONS

```
Statement Of Earnings     ▼ Detach at perforation below and keep for your records ▼
```

1. Ms. Havel works at _____.

    a. Mutual Bank   **b.** Edison Lighting

2. June 1 to June 15 is a _____.

    a. paycheck   **b.** pay period

3. Each month Ms. Havel gets money — her _____.

    a. earnings   **b.** deductions

4. Each month Ms. Havel pays money — her _____.

    a. deductions   **b.** earnings

5. The money she gets <u>before</u> the deductions are taken out is her _____ pay.

    a. gross   **b.** net

6. The money she gets <u>after</u> the deductions are taken out is her _____ pay.

    a. gross   **b.** net

B. Critical thinking. Read the pay stub again. Then answer the questions.

1. How much money has Ms. Havel earned this year? _____

2. How much has she earned this month? _____

3. Which benefit plans has she enrolled in? _____

122   Unit 10

4. How much federal tax did Ms. Havel pay in this pay period? _____

5. How much state tax did she pay in this pay period? _____

6. How many hours did Ms. Havel work in this pay period? _____

Writing

A. Katrin Havel's new husband is a self-employed electrician. He's uninsured, so Ms. Havel enrolls her husband in her medical plan. Read the form. Then answer the questions.

1. How many dependents does Ms. Havel have? _____

2. When did she enroll her husband in the plan? _____

B. Enroll your <u>own</u> dependent in the medical plan.

For extra practice, go to page 148.

➤ Do it yourself!

Discussion. Talk about your own benefits plan, or talk about a friend's or a family member's benefits. Compare benefits with your classmates. Discuss vacation policies, medical and dental plans, and retirement benefits.

Review

A. **Vocabulary. Complete each sentence. Write the words on the line.**

The _____ at this company are terrific! There's a long list of
1. co-payments / benefits

doctors for the _____ plan, and when you visit the doctor, you only
2. medical / retirement

have to pay a small _____. You can retire at age 55 with a good
3. salary / co-payment

_____ and medical benefits for yourself and your _____.
4. salary / pension _5. dependents / benefits_

B. **Conversation. Choose _your_ response. Circle the letter.**

1. "How long have you been self-employed?"
   a. No kidding. **b.** Since early last year.

2. "Guess what!"
   a. What? **b.** Thanks for reminding me.

3. "Long time, no see."
   a. Why don't you get a vision plan? **b.** Hi! How's it going?

C. **Grammar. Complete each sentence with the present perfect.**

1. They ___have been___ in this country since 2000.
   _be_

2. Karl _____ here for two years.
   work

3. She _____ a vacation yet this year.
   not take

4. Marie _____ already _____ her doctor.
   choose

5. _____ you already _____ to Benefits about that?
   speak

D. **Reading and writing. Find the mistake. What is the the correct net pay?** _____

FLORENCIA BAKER		CHECK NO: FW31111	
EARNINGS		**DEDUCTIONS**	
GROSS PAY	$800.50	MEDICAL INSURANCE	$6.30
		DENTAL INSURANCE	$2.40
		FICA	$40.66
		FEDERAL TAX	$90.35
		STATE TAX	$55.20
NET PAY	$665.59	TOTAL DEDUCTIONS	$194.91

Fabric World, Inc.

124   Unit 10

1. Point. Talk about people and things in the office.

    They're talking about benefits plans.

2. Point. Ask questions about the people.

    Has he completed the form yet?

3. Create conversations for the people.

    A: Are there any openings right now?
    B: Yes. Why don't you come in for an interview?

4. Say more about the picture. Use your <u>own</u> words. Say as much as you can.

EDISON LIGHTING
BENEFITS DEPARTMENT

CLAIM FORMS

Edison Lighting Medical Plan

Edison Lighting Dental and Vision Plans

OPENINGS

JULY 17

Benefits Enrollment
Dependent *Hanna Miller*
Relationship *Wife*

Now I can
❑ understand company-paid benefits.
❑ follow company policies.
❑ understand paychecks and pay stubs.

❑ _____.

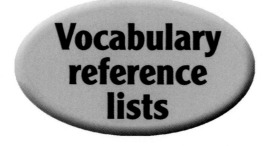

Vocabulary reference lists

This is an alphabetical list of all active vocabulary in *Workplace Plus 2*. The numbers refer to the page on which the word first appears. When a word has two meanings (a new <u>brush</u> OR <u>Brush</u> your hair), both are in the list.

This is a unit-by-unit list of all the social language from the practical conversations in *Workplace Plus 2*.

Welcome to *Workplace Plus*

Hi.
How's it going?
Great.
What about you?
Fine, thanks.
Mary, this is John. John, this is Mary.
Nice to meet you.
Nice to meet you too.
Where are you from?
Me? (for clarification)
And you?
What do you do?
I work in the _____ department.
Well, I have to go now.
Nice meeting you.
See you later.
Excuse me. (to start a conversation)
I'm looking for Mr. Yu.
Mr. Yu? (for clarification)
How do you spell that?
Just a minute.
Oh, yes.
I'm sorry. (to introduce a request)
Could you repeat that, please?
Sure. (to agree to a request)
Thanks.
You're welcome.

Unit 1

Can I help you?
Yes, please.
This is _____. (telephone identification)
I'm calling _____.
Is he in?
Just a moment, please.
It's for you. (to give someone the telephone)
Hello. (telephone greeting)
Is _____ there?
No, I'm sorry. (to express regret)
He's not in right now.

Who's calling?
When will he be back?
I'm not sure.
Would you like to leave a message?
My number's _____.
Oh, hi.
What's it like outside?
By the way, (to introduce a new topic)
Are there any messages for me?

Unit 2

I'm looking for _____.
Well, _____. (to introduce a thought)
How much is _____? (to ask for the cost or price)
$550 a month.
I have a few questions about _____.
Sure. (to respond to a statement or question)
Right around the corner.
What about _____? (to introduce an additional question)
OK. (to agree)
Is there anything else?
It's one month's rent.
That's fine.
No problem.

Unit 3

You can pick it up at about five.
Can you give me an estimate?
It'll be about $50.00. (to give an estimate)
_____ speaking. (to answer the phone)
My _____ aren't working.
What kind of car is it?
That's good for me. (to agree to a suggestion)
I'm here to drop off my car.
What's the problem?
Great! (to respond enthusiastically)
I'll give you a call.

Unit 4

How much is the one over here? (to ask for a price)

Do you have any _____? (to ask for an item in a store)

They're on sale.

They're only $9.99.

That'll be $7.21, please.

This _____ 's on sale for $_____.

I'm sorry, but _____. (to express / introduce an opposing idea / thought / opinion)

That price is for the store brand.

We're sold out.

That's too bad. (to express disappointment)

Will you give me a rain check?

Here you go.

It's good for a month.

I think I was overcharged.

Oh, I'm sorry. (to express regret; to apologize)

Let me have a look.

See, _____. (to show proof)

I'll ring it up again.

Unit 5

One ticket to _____, please.

Round trip or one way?

What's the fare?

When's the next train?

In ten minutes.

At 8:15.

You just missed it.

It left five minutes ago.

Oh, no. (to express disappointment)

They leave every 15 minutes.

Can I still make the 5:22?

Unit 6

Could you please _____? (to ask for a favor)

I'd be glad to.

Anything else?

Thanks for the help.

Anytime. (to respond to a thank-you)

Would you like me to _____? (to offer help)

Thanks for offering, but I can do that myself.

Please let me know if there's anything I can do.

Actually, you could _____. (to accept an offer of help)

I do too.

I'll be right back.

Thanks a million.

Unit 7

I have a question.

What will happen if I make a personal call?

It's against the rules.

You'd better not.

Really? (to express surprise)

Well, thanks for telling me.

That's a good question.

I'd better check with my wife.

Tomorrow's fine.

I just don't get along with my in-laws.

I'm sorry to hear that. (to express sympathy)

You can work it out.

I guess it's worth a try.

Unit 8

Watch out!

What's wrong?

You're right.

Uh-oh.

Good idea.

Me too.

How often should I _____?

Don't forget.

Remember to _____.

Don't worry.

I will.

I won't.

Unit 9

Certainly.
I'm not positive.
I'll check.
I'm interested in getting an ATM card.
Why don't you have a seat?
I'll get you the forms.
How long will it take?
It won't take long.
About a week.
I'll be right with you.
Oops. (to remember something you forgot
    to do)
Just a second.
How would you like that? (to ask about
    monetary denomination)
Let me think....
Twenties, tens, and singles, please.

Unit 10

Yes, I have.
No, I haven't.
Not yet.
We're supposed to do that by 5:00 today.
I know.
Guess what?
What? (as a response to a question)
No kidding. (to show disbelief)
That's terrific.
Immediately.
Long time, no see.
Not great.
I lost my job.
Since March 13.

Irregular verbs

The following verbs from *Workplace Plus 2* have irregular past-tense forms.

Base form	Past-tense form	Past participle
be	was / were	been
break	broke	broken
bring	brought	brought
buy	bought	bought
choose	chose	chosen
come	came	come
do	did	done
drink	drank	drunk
drive	drove	driven
eat	ate	eaten
fall	fell	fallen
fight	fought	fought
find	found	found
forget	forgot	forgotten
get	got	gotten
give	gave	given
go	went	gone
have	had	had
hear	heard	heard
hit	hit	hit
hurt	hurt	hurt
know	knew	known
leave	left	left
let	let	let
lose	lost	lost
make	made	made
mean	meant	meant
meet	met	met
pay	paid	paid
put	put	put
read	read	read
ring	rang	rung
run	ran	run
say	said	said
see	saw	seen
sell	sold	sold
send	sent	sent
speak	spoke	spoken
take	took	taken
tell	told	told
think	thought	thought
understand	understood	understood
wear	wore	worn
withdraw	withdrew	withdrawn
write	wrote	written

State/Possession	Abbreviation	State/Possession	Abbreviation
Alabama	AL	Pennsylvania	PA
Alaska	AK	Puerto Rico	PR
American Samoa	AS	Rhode Island	RI
Arizona	AZ	South Carolina	SC
Arkansas	AR	South Dakota	SD
California	CA	Tennessee	TN
Colorado	CO	Texas	TX
Connecticut	CT	Utah	UT
Delaware	DE	Vermont	VT
District of Columbia	DC	Virgin Islands	VI
Federated States of		Virginia	VA
Micronesia	FM	Washington	WA
Florida	FL	West Virginia	WV
Georgia	GA	Wisconsin	WI
Guam	GU	Wyoming	WY
Hawaii	HI		
Idaho	ID		
Illinois	IL		
Indiana	IN		
Iowa	IA		
Kansas	KS		
Kentucky	KY		
Louisiana	LA		
Maine	ME		
Marshall Islands	MH		
Maryland	MD		
Massachusetts	MA		
Michigan	MI		
Minnesota	MN		
Mississippi	MS		
Missouri	MO		
Montana	MT		
Nebraska	NE		
Nevada	NV		
New Hampshire	NH		
New Jersey	NJ		
New Mexico	NM		
New York	NY		
North Carolina	NC		
North Dakota	ND		
Northern Mariana Islands	MP		
Ohio	OH		
Oklahoma	OK		
Oregon	OR		

Supplementary authentic documents

Use the applications and forms in this section for role plays and more writing practice. Use your <u>own</u> words and ideas.

To _____

Date _____ Time _____ A.M. ☐ P.M. ☐

WHILE YOU WERE OUT

M _____

Phone _____

Area code   Number   Extension

☐ telephoned   ☐ please call
☐ returned your call ☐ will call back

Message _____

_____

_____

_____

_____

_____

Brookside Realty
SALES COMMISSION & FEE AGREEMENT

Name: _____

Name: _____

Address: _____

Phone: (H) (_____) _____-_____ (W) (_____) _____-_____

Annual Income: _____ **Desired Date of Occupancy:** _____

Price Range: _____-_____

Type of Unit: Condo – 1 Br. 2 Br. 3 Br.   1 Fam.   2 Fam.   Multi Fam.

We, BROOKSIDE REALTY, agree to introduce you to various dwellings so that you
may purchase one. You agree that any dwellings introduced to you by BROOKSIDE
REALTY for sale, you will purchase, make offers to purchase, or have negotiations
of any kind only through BROOKSIDE REALTY on these dwellings. If you
negotiate the purchase through any other broker on a property introduced to you
through BROOKSIDE REALTY, and the seller or other broker does not pay
BROOKSIDE REALTY'S commission, you may be held liable for said commission. I
(We) agree that if BROOKSIDE REALTY is forced to take legal action as a result of
a breach of this agreement, and BROOKSIDE REALTY is the prevailing party, I (we)
will be responsible for any legal fees incurred by BROOKSIDE REALTY. I (We) have
read and agreed to the aforementioned terms and conditions.

THIS IS A LEGAL AND BINDING AGREEMENT. PLEASE READ IT CAREFULLY
BEFORE SIGNING. PLEASE REQUEST A COPY.

Signature: _____ **Date:** _____

Signature: _____ **Date:** _____

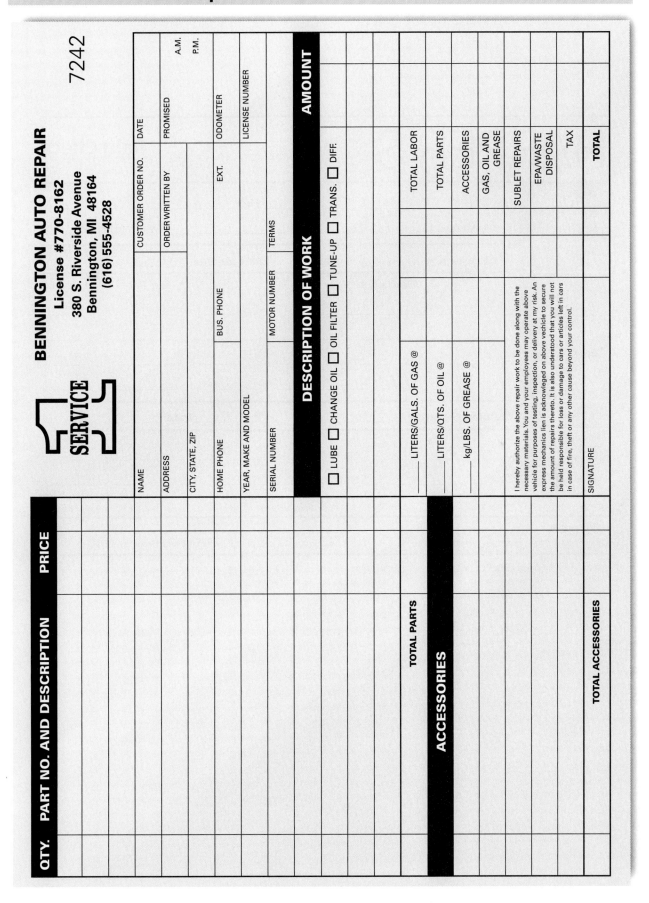

HARPER'S   **Rain Check**

Customer Information:	Last Name: _____ First: _____ Phone Number: _____ Date: _____ Associate Initials: _____

✓	☑ Store Rain check ☐ Request Total # of Cards: _____

	SKU/Description	Qty.	Reg. Price	Sale Price
Item (s):	_____	_____	_____	_____
	_____	_____	_____	_____
	_____	_____	_____	_____
	_____	_____	_____	_____

Pick-Up:	**Customer Signature:** _____ **Date:** _____

Contact Information:	Date: _____ Comments: _____ Date: _____ Comments: _____

SKU# 9018572   Customer copy   Rev 5/00

RAIN CHECKS
Rain checks are not a guarantee of future availability. A rain check assures you the sale price if / when the item becomes available.

MAIL & GO APPLICATION   Metro-South Railroad

OFFICIAL USE ONLY

Personal Data (Must Complete)

PLEASE PRINT   Mr. /Mrs./Ms. (circle one)   Sex: ☐ Male   ☐ Female

Last Name: First Name: MI:

Mailing Address:

City: State: Zip: —

Home Telephone: Business Telephone:

AREA CODE   AREA CODE

Employer Name:

Employer Address: City: State: Zip:

Travel Information (Must Complete)

Original Station: Destination Station:

UniPass Station: Bus Provider/Route #:

Receive no value on CityCard, or choose:

☐ **$54 Mail & Go *Plus* (*Unlimited* monthly travel; 9% rail fare discount applies)** Value expires at end of month; value cannot be transferred to another CityCard.

☐ **$50 Mail & Go *Plus* (44 rides; 9% rail fare discount applies)** Value expires at end of month; value cannot be transferred to another CityCard.

☐ **$20 (22 rides; no rail fare discount) Card good for one year** and value can be transferred to another CityCard at any subway station.

Payment Options (Choose One of Three Options Below)

❶ CREDIT CARD OPTION

Please charge the following credit card automatically on the third of each month:

☐ MasterCard ☐ VISA ☐ American Express ☐ Discover

Credit Card Number:

Expiration Date: —

Print Name of Authorized Cardholder: (as it appears on Credit Card)

Credit Card Billing Address (if different from above mailing address)

I hereby apply for a monthly Mail & Go Ticket and for automatic payment to be made with the above-noted credit card. By signing below I agree to the terms and conditions printed to the left and reverse side of this form for this payment option.

Signature of Authorized Card Holder   Date

❷ PRE-AUTHORIZED DEBIT OPTION

Please debit the following checking account automatically on the third of each month:

Bank Name:

Checking Account Number:

Offical Use:

Name on account: (Both names if joint account. Please print)

PLACE CHECK HERE

Please enclose voided check from Checking Account in pouch provided **here** ⟶

I hereby apply for a monthly Mail & Go Ticket and for automatic payment to be debited from the above-noted checking account. By signing below I agree to the terms and conditions printed to the left and reverse side of this form for this payment option.

Signature   Date

Signature (joint account)   Date

❸ PAYMENT BY CHECK OPTION: ☐ Check Here

I hereby apply for a monthly Mail & Go Ticket. (I agree to pay for my ticket so that payment is received by Metro-South Commuter Railroad by the third day of the month for which the ticket is valid. I will not deduct credits from the invoice amount, and agree to the conditions of use printed to the left and reverse side of this form.)

Signature   Date

TEAR AT PERFORATION AND MOISTEN SEAL

Lodging

Address: //traveler'schoicehotel.com/supplychecklist/   go

[back] [forward] [stop] [refresh] [home] [print] [mail]

▌ Traveler's Choice Hotel ▌
Supply Checklist

Room Supplies

.75 oz. Shampoo Bottle	#SHMP1.247	$42.72/288	☐
.25 oz. Shampoo Packet	#SHMP1.07	$35.48/500	☐
3/4 Wrapped Facial Soap	#SP6A	$49.90/1000	☐
1.5 Wrapped Deodorant Soap	#D-SP125	$42.90/500	☐
Green/Yellow Scrub Sponge	#SPNG374	$20.69/20	☐
Foaming Disinfectant Bathroom Clnr	#DISCLNR88	$1.23/qt	☐
Glass Cleaner	#GLSCLNR108	$1.24/qt	☐
Bleach	#BLCH53	$6.76/6gal	☐
Rubber Glove	#RUBGLV446	$5.89/12	☐
2 ply Toilet Tissue	#TLTTIS06	$29.99/96	☐
Facial Tissue	#FACTIS30	$12.93/30	☐

Breakfast Bar Supplies

Plastic Knife	#PLASKNF64	$6.46/1000	☐
Plastic Teaspoon	#PLASTSP68	$6.46/1000	☐
Regular In Room Coffee	#REGCOF987	$27.72/150	☐
Decaf In Room Coffee	#DECCOF988	$30.46/150	☐
Creamer Packet	#CRMRPK002	$10.63/1000	☐
Assorted Jelly	#ASRTJLY48	$4.99/200	☐
Sugar Packet	#SGRPK31	$7.94/2000	☐
Teabag	#TEABG41	$2.76/1000	☐
Beverage Napkin	#BEVNAP200	$13.68/1000	☐
6" Paper Plate	#6-PPRPLT206	$6.73/1000	☐

For first time and existing customers:
Customer's Name ____   E-mail address ____
Shipping Address   Phone Number ____
Street ____
City, State ZIP ____

For existing Dover customers:
Dover Customer Number ____ (if applicable)
Delivery Day ____ (if applicable)
Salesperson's Name ____ (if applicable)

All orders for existing Dover Customers should be submitted to Dover by Thursday for delivery on Wednesday, Thursday, or Friday of the following week. Prices are subject to change based on market conditions.

[**Submit the form**] [**Clear all fields**]

U.S. HealthFirst
HEALTH CLAIM TRANSMITTAL

Employee Name: _____ SSN: ____ - ____ - ____ Date of Birth: ____ / ____ / ____

Employee Address: _____ Check if New Address ❏

Employee Phone Number: (____) _____ Status: ❏ Active ❏ Retired ❏ Continued (COBRA)
_ _ _ _ _ _ _ _ _ _ _ Area Code _ _ _ _ _ _ Number

Spouse Name: _____ Spouse Date of Birth: ____ / ____ / ____

Patient Name: _____ Patient Date of Birth: ____ / ____ / ____ Relationship: _____

Nature of Illness or Injury: _____

_____

IF CLAIM IS DUE TO INJURY STATE WHEN, WHERE AND HOW INJURY OCCURRED

Do You Have More Than One Employer?   Yes ❏   No ❏

Is Your Spouse Employed?   Yes ❏   No ❏

Is Patient Employed?   Yes ❏   No ❏
If you answered "yes" to any of the above questions, please provide the following information:

Employed Person: _____ Social Security Number: ____ - ____ - ____

Employer: _____

Employer Address: _____ Phone Number: (____) _____
_ Area Code _ _ _ _ Number

Insurance Company & Policy Number: _____

ANY PERSON WHO KNOWINGLY FILES A STATEMENT OF CLAIM CONTAINING ANY MISREPRESENTATION OR ANY FALSE, INCOMPLETE OR MISLEADING INFORMATION MAY BE GUILTY OF A CRIMINAL ACT PUNISHABLE UNDER LAW AND MAY BE SUBJECT TO CIVIL PENALTIES.

Employee Signature: _____ Date: ____ / ____ / ____

HINTS FOR SUBMITTING CLAIMS TO U.S. HEALTHFIRST

- If you want U.S. HealthFirst to pay benefits directly to the provider of medical services,

  Please sign here _____

- Attach your bills to this completed form and mail to U.S. HealthFirst.
- Make sure all bills indicate the reason (diagnosis) for treatment and list the date, type and cost of each service.
- Send additional bills periodically or when they total $50.00 or more.

For U.S. HealthFirst USE ONLY

DATE BENEFITS BECAME EFFECTIVE						DATE BENEFITS TERMINATED						SUFFIX	ACCOUNT
MO	DAY	YR	MO	DAY	YR	MO	DAY	YR	MO	DAY	YR		
Emp.			Dep.			Emp.			Dep.				

SIGNATURE OF U.S. HEALTHFIRST EMPLOYEE CERTIFYING BENEFITS:	DATE	MO	DAY	YR

NORTH PARK CHILDCARE CENTER

APPLICATION FOR EMPLOYMENT

POSITION DESIRED _____ DATE _____

HOW DID YOU LEARN OF OUR ORGANIZATION? _____

HOURS YOU ARE AVAILABLE TO WORK: <u>Mon</u>   <u>Tues</u>   <u>Wed</u>   <u>Thur</u>   <u>Fri</u>   <u>Sat</u>   <u>Sun</u>

From: _____

☐ Full-Time   ☐ Part-Time   ☐ On-Call   To: _____

I.

NAME _____ SS NUMBER _____
     Last   First   Middle

ADDRESS _____
        Street   City   State   Zip Code

TELEPHONE NO. _____ If necessary, best time to call you at home _____

HAVE YOU EVER FILED AN APPLICATION WITH OR BEEN EMPLOYED BY A DIVISION OF NPCC

BEFORE? _____ If yes, give date(s) _____

ARE YOU CERTIFIED TO PERFORM INFANT OR TODDLER CPR? _____

ARE YOU LEGALLY ELIGIBLE FOR EMPLOYMENT IN THE UNITED STATES?_____
(Proof of U.S. Citizenship or immigration status will be required upon employment)

HAVE YOU EVER BEEN CONVICTED OF A MISDEMEANOR OR A FELONY IN ANY JURISDICTION?

_____ If yes, describe in detail: _____

_____

II. Employment Experience

A. EMPLOYER _____ Address _____

Dates of Employment _____ Salary _____

Telephone No. _____ Supervisor _____

Describe your work _____

Why did you leave? _____

May we contact this employer? _____ Yes _____ No

Please complete the entire application in blue or black ink to ensure the fastest response.

Please show us how you would like your name to appear on the Card.
Please spell the last name completely. (Full name must not exceed 20 spaces.)

Personal Information

(Optional) ☐ Mr. ☐ Mrs. ☐ Miss ☐ Ms. ☐ Dr.

			Mo. Day Yr.

First, Middle, Last Name (Please print above) — Date of Birth

Home Address (Apt. #, if any) — City — State — Zip

Yrs.   Mos.   (   )   –   –

Time at Current Address   Home Phone   Social Security Number   E-Mail Address (optional)

$ _____ $ _____

Annual Personal Gross Income   Additional Personal Income*   Source of Additional Income†

☐ Own Home   *Minimum Personal Yearly Income–$15,000
☐ Rent   †Include salary, income from savings and source (banker, broker, employer, etc.) whom we can call for confirmation
                 (alimony, separate maintenance, or child support need not be revealed if you do not wish to rely on it.)

Business and Financial Information

	( )

Employer or Firm Name   Business Phone

Business Street Address   City   State   Zip

Yrs.   Mos.   ☐ Full-Time Student ☐ Self-Employed ☐ Retired

Position at Firm   Time There

Do you have any of the following?
Checking Account ☐ Yes ☐ No   Savings Account (includes Money Market, CD) ☐ Yes ☐ No

☐ Major/Other Credit Card ☐ Department Store/Retail ☐ Gas/Oil

Bank Name

Please sign below.

Additional information may be requested by us for further
processing when you apply with this form. By signing below,
I certify that I have read, met, and agreed to all of the terms,
conditions, and disclosures on this application.

X _____
Signature of Applicant (Please do not print.)   Date

Please fill in the following to obtain an Additional Card.

For $30 a year you can obtain an Additional Card for qualified individuals age
18 or older.

First, Middle, Last Name (Please print.)

Month   Day   Year | –   –

Date of Birth   Social Security Number

HMO Enrollment/Change Application

HMO Name	HMO Plan State	HMO Coverage Category	HMO Group/Policy Number	Division	Location	Coverage Effective Date
		☐ Employee Only ☐ Employee +1 ☐ Employee + Family				

Employee Last Name	First Name	MI	Hire Date	Birth Date	Sex ☐ Male ☐ Female	Marital Status ☐ Single ☐ Married ☐ Separated ☐ Divorced	Social Security Number

Street Address (Must Live in HMO Service Area)		City	State	Zip	Country

Employee Status
☐ Active   ☐ COBRA   ☐ Retiree

Type of Enrollment
☐ Open Enrollment   ☐ New Hire

☐ Change: Life Status Change ___ Relocation/Transfer ___ Other ___

Home Phone ( )   Work Phone ( )

Eligible Dependents

Full Name (First, MI, Last)	Birth Date (mm/dd/yy)	Sex (M/F)	Relationship	Social Security Number	College Name and Location (For Full-time College Students)	Choice of Primary Care Physician or Health Center	Physician/ Center Code
	/ /		self				
	/ /		spouse				
	/ /						
	/ /						
	/ /						
	/ /						

Dentist (if applicable) _____ Code _____

Pharmacy (if applicable) _____ Code _____

Information About Other Medical Coverage

Do you, your spouse, or any enrolled dependents have Medicare coverage?
☐ Yes   ☐ No

If yes, show for whom   ☐ Self   ☐ Spouse   ☐ Dependent name _____

Medicare No./Health Ins. No. (Claim No.) _____

Effective Dates: Part A ___ / / ___   Part B ___ / / ___

Do your spouse or dependents have other group hospital medical insurance?
☐ Yes   ☐ No

Covered Member Name(s) _____

Employer Name _____

Employer Address _____

Employer Phone _____

Insurance Company Name _____

Policy Group Member _____

ENROLLMENT AGREEMENT AND PAYROLL DEDUCTION AUTHORIZATION

I certify that I have reviewed all of the statements in this application and that they are true and complete. I apply for coverage with the HMO indicated above for the person(s) listed on this form. I agree that I and all my eligible dependents shall abide by the provisions of coverage in the service agreement of the HMO under which we are enrolled. The subscriber contract which I am issued will determine the rights and responsibilities of member(s) and will govern in the event of conflicts with any benefits comparison or summary description of the HMO Plan.

On behalf of myself and my eligible dependents, I hereby authorize all hospitals, physicians, and medical service providers and other organizations (including insurers and any prepaid health plan) to give the HMO (or its representative) access to relevant medical, prescription drug, employment, and insurance coverage records. I understand that both on my behalf, and on behalf of my eligible dependents, as a condition for the receipt of benefits and services, the above mentioned entities have the right to share and review these records.

This information will be utilized by the HMO to verify services performed for me and my eligible dependents, and also for utilization review and quality assurance, this authorization shall remain valid for the term of this coverage.

EMPLOYEE SIGNATURE: _____   DATE: _____

Grammar Booster ➤

UNIT 1

1. Will and won't for the future: statements

Subject	will / won't	Base form of the verb	
I We You They He She It	will won't	be	here soon.

Contractions
I + will = I'**ll**
We + will = we'**ll**
you + will = you'**ll**
they + will = they'**ll**
he + will = he'**ll**
she + will = she'**ll**
it + will = it'**ll**
will + not = **won't**

Thing to remember
Be careful! Don't use to after will.

She will call.
NOT She will to call.

A. Write sentences with **will**. Use contractions.

1. _Mr. D'Amico won't be at work tomorrow._
   Mr. D'Amico / not / be at work tomorrow

2. _____
   You / need a coat tonight

3. _____
   We / not / have time for coffee

4. _____
   The weather / not / be good this weekend

5. _____
   I / call the manager

2. Will in yes / no questions and short answers

Will	Subject	Base form of the verb	
Will	I you we they he she it	need	more time?

Short answers		
Yes,	you I we they he she it	will.
No,		won't.

Unit 1   **GB-1**

B. Complete the questions with <u>will</u> and the words given. Write the short answers.

1. **A:** <u>Will you eat</u> _____ lunch outside today?
   you / eat

   B: _____. I never eat outside.

2. **A:** _____ the phones?
   Ms. Chen / answer

   B: _____. She always answers the phones.

3. **A:** _____ to the movie with us?
   they / go

   B: _____. They have to study.

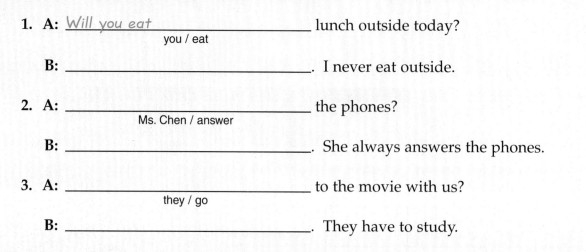

3. <u>Will</u> in information questions

Question word	<u>will</u>	Subject	Base form of the verb		Answers
What time	will	we	**have**	dinner?	At 7:00.
When		she	**be**	home?	Later tonight.

Thing to remember
Sometimes the question word is the subject.
Who will fix the sink?

C. Look at Jack's list of things he will do. Complete the information questions. Use <u>will</u>.

> Go shopping at Best Foods at 10:00. Buy
>
> chicken, rice, salad, soda
>
> Take car to Rick's Auto repair at 2:00
>
> Call Mom tonight

1. **A:** <u>Where will Jack go shopping?</u> _____

   B: At Best Foods.

2. **A:** _____?

   B: Chicken, rice, salad, and soda.

3. **A:** _____?

   B: At 2:00.

4. **A:** _____?

   B: His mother.

4. Object pronouns <u>me</u>, <u>you</u>, <u>him</u>, <u>her</u>, and <u>us</u>

	Object pronoun
I need some help with this. Can you help	**me**?
You have to call her. She left a message for	**you**.
Ana came to see you. Please call	**her**.
Mr. Lee went to lunch. Do you want to wait for	**him**?
We're going out. Do you want to come with	**us**?

Things to remember
1. Use object pronouns after verbs:
I'll **call her**. We don't **need him**.
2. Use object pronouns after <u>for</u>, <u>to</u>, and <u>with</u>:
Sit next **to me**. Come **with us**.

D. **Choose the subject pronoun or the object pronoun. Write it on the line.**

1. Please take a message for _*him*_.

he / him

2. _____ always eat lunch at 12:00.

We / Us

3. The weather is cool. Bring a jacket for _____.

she / her

4. _____ worked with us for two years.

He / Him

5. The teacher wants to talk to _____ in her office.

we / us

6. I'll call _____ tonight.

he / him

E. **Complete each sentence with an object pronoun.**

1. Our parents always took _____*us*_____ to school.

my sister and I

2. We like Mr. Santos. We have lunch with _____ every day.

Mr. Santos

3. I have a message for your mother. Please give this message to _____.

your mother

4. Are there any messages for _____?

you and me

5. I'll be home tonight. Please call _____.

I

6. Ms. Wilson needs help. Let's help _____.

Ms. Wilson

7. Is that your brother? I know _____. He's in my class.

your brother

8. Our teacher gave _____ new books.

the other students and I

5. Would like to + verb in statements

Subject	Would like to	Base form of the verb	
I We You They He She	would like to	go	to lunch.

Things to remember

1. Contractions:
   I + would = I'd
   we + would = we'd
   you + would = you'd
   they + would = they'd
   he + would = he'd
   she + would = she'd

2. Use the base form of the verb after would like to.

3. I'd like is often a more polite way to say I want.
   I want to eat lunch.
   I'd like to eat lunch.

F. Write the sentences with **would like to**. Use contractions if possible.

1. _I'd like to buy this umbrella._
   I / buy this umbrella

2. _____
   He / go to a movie

3. _____
   Mr. and Mrs. Cho / stay home

4. _____
   We / talk to the manager

5. _____
   I / eat outside

6. Would like to + verb in yes / no questions and short answers

Would	Subject	like to	Base form of the verb	
Would	you they she	like to	work	there?

Short answers		
Yes,	I they	would.
No,	she	wouldn't.

G. Complete the conversations. Use **would like to**.

1. **A:** _Would you like to_ have a hot drink? Coffee or tea?

   B: Yes, _____. I'd like coffee, please.

2. **A:** _____ eat lunch now?

   B: No, _____. We aren't hungry.

3. **A:** _____ leave a message?

   B: Yes, _____. He'd like to leave a message for Tom Baker.

Question word	would	Subject	like to	Base form of the verb		Answers
What		you		**do**?		I'd like to have some coffee.
When	would	they	like to	**eat**?		At 6:00 p.m.
Where		he		**go**?		To China.

H. Write information questions with <u>would like to</u>.

1. **A:** <u>What would Ms. Perez like to do?</u>
   What / Ms. Perez / do

   B: She'd like to study English.

2. **A:** _____?
   When / they / leave

   B: At 10:15.

3. **A:** _____?
   Where / Patrick / work

   B: At a bank.

4. **A:** _____?
   What / you / do

   B: Go shopping.

U N I T   2

1. Object pronouns <u>it</u> and <u>them</u>

	Object pronoun	
Please fix **the phones**. We need to use	**them**.	
The Garcias are back from Tampa. I talked to	**them**	last night.
My wife paid **the rent** last month. I paid	**it**	this month.
Who paid for **dinner**? Did you pay for	**it**?	

Things to remember
1. Use object pronouns after verbs or after <u>for</u>, <u>to</u>, and <u>with</u>.
2. Use <u>it</u> for a thing. Use <u>them</u> for people or things.

A. Complete the sentences. Write <u>it</u> or <u>them</u>.

1. It's a nice apartment. I like ___it___.

2. Where are my keys? Do you have _____?

3. This wallet is too small. I won't buy _____.

4. The Chuns lived in Apartment 2B, and the Smiths lived next to _____.

5. This is a great neighborhood. I love _____!

Unit 2   **GB-5**

	Verb	Object (noun/pronoun)	to / for	Object (noun/pronoun)
The manager	gave	the keys **them**	**to**	Manuel. **him**.
She	signed	the paychecks **them**	**for**	Jin and me. **us**.
I	read	the ad **it**	**to**	Mr. and Mrs. Kelly. **them**.

B. Write two sentences: (a) use two nouns, and (b) use two object pronouns.

1. I gave the to .

   Mr. Gale

   a. <u>I gave the checkbook to Mr. Gale.</u>

   b. <u>I gave it to him.</u>

2. We'll pay the _____ for _____.

   Ms. Moreno

   a. _____

   b. _____

3. Please give the _____ to _____.

   the Mees

   a. _____

   b. _____

4. She signed the _____ for _____.

   John

   a. _____

   b. _____

UNIT 3

1. It and them with two-word verbs

With nouns			With it / them			
I'd like to	**pick up**	**my car**.	I'd like to	**pick**	**it**	**up**.
Please	**turn on**	**your headlights**.	Please	**turn**	**them**	**on**.

A. Complete the sentences. Write it or them.

1. The light is on. Please turn __*it*__ off.

2. My headlights don't work. I can't turn _____ on.

3. Bring your car in at 8:00 and drop _____ off.

4. Their cars are ready. They can pick _____ up.

5. I need gas. Please fill _____ up.

6. I don't want to watch TV. Please turn _____ off.

B. Complete the conversations. Use words from the boxes and it or them.

~~drop off~~	fill up	pick up	turn on	turn off

1. **A:** Al's Repair Shop. Al speaking.

   B: Hello. My TV and VCR aren't working. Can I _____*drop them off*_____
   today?

2. **A:** Why are your headlights on?

   B: I always drive with my headlights on. I never _____.

3. **A:** We need gas.

   B: There's a gas station. Let's _____.

4. **A:** Hello. This is Carla Bianco. Is my car ready?

   B: Yes, it is. Would you like to _____ now?

5. **A:** Can we listen to the radio?

   B: No, the baby is sleeping. Don't _____.

Subject	be	Verb + -ing
I	was	
He		
She		working.
It		
We	were	
You		
They		

Subject	be	not	Verb + -ing
I	was		
He			
She		not	working.
It			
We	were		
You			
They			

Things to remember
1. The past continuous is made of two parts:
(1) <u>was</u> or <u>were</u> and
(2) verb + <u>-ing</u>.
2. You can use contractions:
was + not = **wasn't**
were + not = **weren't**

10:00   11:00   12:00

was working   Now

C. **Complete the sentences. Use the past continuous. Use contractions.**

1. We had a problem with our TV last week. It _wasn't working_.

                                        not / work

2. Ann was at the auto parts store. She _____ windshield wipers.

                                                      buy

3. The mechanics were at work, but they _____ cars.

                                             not / fix

4. Mr. Yee hurt his back last night. He _____ a tire on his car.

                                             change

5. I _____, but you _____!

       talk   not / listen

Be	Subject	Verb + -ing
Was	I	
	he	
	she	
	it	helping?
Were	we	
	you	
	they	

Short answers							
Yes,	you	**were.**		No,	you	**weren't.**
	he				he	
	she	**was.**			she	**wasn't.**
	it				it	
	you				you	
	we	**were.**			we	**weren't.**
	they				they	

D. What were these people doing at 5:30 yesterday? Complete the conversations.

1. **Helen**

   A: _Was Helen talking_ _____ to her mechanic?
   <u>talk</u>

   B: _Yes, she was._ _____

2. **Gary**

   A: _____ the tires on his car?
   <u>change</u>

   B: _____. He was checking the oil.

3. **Janelle**

   A: _____ her hair?
   <u>wash</u>

   B: _____.

4. **the Tangs**

   A: _____ dinner?
   <u>eat</u>

   B: _____. They _____.

4. The past continuous: information questions

Question word	<u>be</u>	Subject	Verb + <u>-ing</u>		Answers
What	**were**	you	**doing**	at 8:00?	I was reading.
What kind of car	**was**	he	**fixing**?		An SUV.

Thing to remember
Sometimes the question word is the subject.
Who was driving the truck?

E. Complete the conversations with the past continuous.

1. **A:** Hiro left 10 minutes ago. _Where was he going?_ _____
   Where / he / go

   B: To the store.

2. **A:** Tony and Maria were in a car accident, but they're OK.

   B: _____?
   Who / drive

   A: Tony.

3. **A:** I didn't answer the phone. I was busy.

   B: _____?
   What / you / do

   A: I was washing my car.

4. **A:** Tim and Robin were at Herb's Autos last night. They were buying a car.

   B: _____?
   What kind of car / they / buy

   A: A used car.

5. The past continuous and the simple past tense

Subject	Past continuous		When	Subject	Simple past	
I	**was cleaning**	the kitchen	**when**	he	**called**	me.
They	**were driving**	home		the warning light	**went**	on.

F. Complete the paragraph. Write the past continuous or the simple past tense.

I ___*was driving*___ to the supermarket when it _____ to rain.
      1. drive   2. start

When I _____ my windshield wipers, they made a funny sound.
                    3. turn on

So I _____ my cell phone to call my brother. He _____ TV
              4. use   5. watch

when I _____, but he said, "Come on over and I'll look at them."
                6. call

U N I T   4

1. Comparisons with adjectives: comparatives

- To form the comparative of short (usually, one-syllable*) adjectives, add –er to the adjective. Here are some spelling rules:
  1. For most adjectives, add –er.
     cheap → cheap**er**   small → small**er**
  2. For adjectives ending in e, add –r only.
     nice → nice**r**   large → large**r**
  3. For adjectives ending in y, change y to i and add –er.
     busy → bus**ier**   early → earl**ier**
  4. For adjectives ending in a consonant, vowel, and consonant, double the final consonant and add –er.
     hot → hot**ter**   thin → thin**ner**
- To form the comparative of most adjectives with two or more syllables, add more before the adjective.
     expensive → **more expensive**   interesting → **more** interesting
- A few adjectives are irregular.
     good → better   bad → worse
- When comparing two things, use the word than.
     This bottle of shampoo is **larger than** that bottle.
     This shampoo is **more expensive than** that one.

*A syllable is a word or part of a word with one vowel sound: cheap has one syllable; busy has two syllables.

A. **Complete the sentences. Use the comparative form of the adjective and <u>than</u>.**

1. The River Apartments are ____*nicer than*____ the apartments in my building.

nice

2. My class is _____ your class.

early

3. Union Supermarket is _____ Grand Food Store.

good

4. The schools in that neighborhood are _____ the schools in our

bad
   neighborhood.

5. Here you go. This coffee is _____ the coffee in that cup.

hot

6. Are you _____ your brother?

old

7. Is this car _____ that car?

cheap

B. **Complete the sentences. Use a comparative form of <u>beautiful</u>, <u>expensive</u>, or <u>interesting</u> and <u>than</u>.**

1. **A:** How did you like the new book?

   B: It was _____*more interesting*_____ than the last one.

2. **A:** This apartment is beautiful.

   B: You have to see the apartment across the hall.

   It's _____ this one!

3. **A:** Do you like your new job? Is it interesting?

   B: It's not bad. It's _____ my last job.

4. **A:** Is Quick Mart expensive?

   B: It's _____ Bell Foods, but I like it because it's
   around the corner.

5. **A:** This park is really beautiful.

   B: Yes, but Grant Park is _____ this park. It's my
   favorite park!

C. Write comparisons. Use the comparative forms of <u>cheap</u>, <u>dirty</u>, <u>expensive</u>, or <u>good</u>.

1. The red car <u>is cheaper than the green car</u>.
   _{cheap}

2. The kitchen floor _____.
   _{dirty}

3. The small box _____.
   _{expensive}

4. The new TV _____.
   _{good}

---

2. <u>One</u> / <u>ones</u> and questions with <u>which</u>

<u>Which</u>	Noun			Answers
	hair dryer	is better?		The larger **one**.
Which	**TV**	did you buy?		The **one** on sale.
	cameras	are on sale?		The **ones** on that shelf.

D. Ask a question with <u>which</u>.

1. A: <u>Which painkiller is better?</u>
      _{better}
   B: No-Pain.

2. A: _____?
      _{cheaper}
   B: The tissues in the blue box.

3. A: _____?
      _{expensive}
   B: Bright White.

4. A: _____?
      _{on sale}
   B: The AA batteries.

E. Complete the conversations. Write <u>one</u> or <u>ones</u>.

1. **A:** Which drugstore do you like?

    B: The ___one___ on the corner of High Street.

2. **A:** Which toothbrushes are on sale this week?

    B: The _____ over there, next to the door.

3. **A:** Here are two cameras. Which _____ would you like?

    B: The smaller _____.

4. **A:** Why did you buy a new hair dryer?

    B: Our old _____ doesn't work.

U N I T 5

1. <u>Should</u> / <u>shouldn't</u>: Statements

Subject	should / shouldn't	Base form of the verb	
I We You They He She It	should	leave	early.
	shouldn't		

Things to remember

1. Use <u>should</u> or <u>shouldn't</u> to give advice.
   You **should** be on time for work.
   You **shouldn't** arrive late.

2. You can use contractions:
   should + not = **shouldn't**.

3. Be careful! Don't use <u>to</u> after <u>should</u>.
   He should go.
   NOT He should to go.

A. Complete the sentences. Use <u>should</u> or <u>shouldn't</u>.

1. _You shouldn't take_____ the express. It doesn't stop at Broadway.
   You / not / take

2. Let's leave soon. _____ late.
   We / not / be

3. Ivan's car is old. _____ a new one.
   He / get

4. _____ a train. It's faster than the bus.
   They / take

5. _____ this car. It's too large.
   We / not / buy

6. My daughter has a fever. I think _____ the doctor.
   I / call

2. Should: <u>yes</u> / <u>no</u> questions and short answers

Should	Subject	Base form of the verb	
Should	I we Mr. Lee	**take**	the bus?

Short answers						
Yes,	you we he	**should**.	No,	you we he	**shouldn't**.

B. Put the words in order. Complete the conversations.

1. **A:** *Should I take the local?*

   I / Should / the local / take

   B: No, _____. Take the express. It's faster.

2. **A:** _____?

   buy / I / my ticket / Should

   B: Yes, _____. And you should hurry!

3. **A:** _____?

   a taxi / Should / take / we

   B: No, _____. Taxis are too expensive. Let's take the bus.

3. Should: information questions

Question word	should	Subject	Base form of the verb		Answers
What		she	**do**?		She should take the train.
When	**should**	we	**leave**?		In 15 minutes.
Which bus		I	**take**?		The one to San Pedro.

C. Complete the conversations. Write information questions with <u>should</u> and <u>what</u>, <u>when</u>, <u>where</u>, or <u>why</u>.

1. **A:** *Where should he go?*

   go

   B: To the doctor's office.

2. **A:** _____?

   take his medicine

   B: At 9:00 tonight.

3. **A:** _____?

   stay home

   B: Because she has a fever.

4. **A:** _____?

   take

   B: A painkiller, like aspirin.

4. Could / couldn't: statements

Subject	could / couldn't	Base form of the verb	
I We You	**could**		
They		**go**	by bus or train.
He She It	**couldn't**		

Things to remember
1. Use <u>could</u> to say that something is possible:
You **could** pay cash, or you **could** write a check.
2. You can use contractions:
could + not = **couldn't**
3. Be careful! Don't use <u>to</u> after <u>could</u>.
They could take the early train. NOT ~~They could to take the early train.~~

D. Complete the conversations. Use <u>could</u> and the words given.

1. **A:** We just missed the 7:15!

   B: But _____ *we could make* _____ the 7:25.

              we / make

2. **A:** When's the next train to Hot Springs?

   B: _____ the 7:30 express.

           we / take

3. **A:** Sara just called. She missed the bus.

   B: _____ her home.

           I / drive

4. **A:** I have to get coffee. Do we have time?

   B: _____ your ticket for you. Then we'll have time.

           I / buy

   A: Great! Thanks!

5. **A:** Let's go to a movie. We could see <u>The Last Cowboy</u> at 7:00 or 9:00.

   B: _____ the 7:00 show or the 9:00 show.

           I / make

5. Could: <u>yes</u> / <u>no</u> questions and short answers

Could	Subject	Base form of the verb	
Could	I we she	**take**	the 1:10 bus?

Short answers						
Yes,	you we she	**could.**	No,	you we she	**couldn't.**

E. Complete the <u>yes</u> / <u>no</u> questions. Use <u>could</u> and <u>take</u>. Look at the schedule and write answers.

READING LINE Blue numbers = Express trains

North Station	Everett	Malden	Melrose	Reading
7:15	7:30	8:00	8:30	9:00
7:25	7:40	--------	--------	8:40
7:30	7:45	8:15	8:45	9:15
7:30	--------	8:05	--------	8:55

1. **A:** Nancy needs to go to Everett. _Could she take_ the 7:15 train?

   B: _Yes, she could_ .

2. **A:** Mr. Delacroix needs to go to Malden. _____ the 7:25?

   B: _____ .

3. **A:** Linda and Pete need to go to Melrose. _____ the 7:30 express?

   B: _____ . But they could take the local.

4. **A:** I need to go to Reading. _____ an express train?

   B: _____ .

---

6. <u>Could</u> in information questions

Question word	could	Subject	Base form of the verb		Answers
When	could	we	go	shopping?	On Saturday or Sunday.
Which trains		I	take?		You could take the 7:15 or the 7:35.

F. Complete the conversations. Write information questions with <u>could</u> and <u>what</u>, <u>when</u>, <u>where</u>, and <u>which</u>.

1. **A:** Let's go out to eat tonight. _Where could we go?_

   go

   B: Well, we could go to Nini's, or we could try the new Chinese restaurant.

2. **A:** I need to arrive in Springfield before 9:00. _____?

   take

   B: You could take the local train at 8:00 or the express at 8:20.

3. **A:** Miguel has a headache. _____?

   take

   B: I have aspirin and another painkiller. He could take either one.

4. **A:** I'd like to leave early tomorrow. _____?

   be

   B: I could be ready at 7:00.

1. Agreeing with <u>too</u> and <u>either</u>: simple present tense

AFFIRMATIVE	
They **like** this neighborhood.	I **do too**.
He **has** a job.	She **does too**.
We **need supplies**.	They **do too**.

Things to remember
She has a job. I have a job too. = I do too.
She doesn't like her job. I don't like my job either.
= I don't either.

NEGATIVE	
They **don't like** this neighborhood.	I **don't either**.
He **doesn't have** a job.	She **doesn't either**.
We **don't need supplies**.	They **don't either**.

A. **Complete the conversations. Use <u>too</u> or <u>either</u>.**

1. **A:** I need a sponge.

   B: *I do too.* _____
   I

2. **A:** I have to work tomorrow.

   B: _____
   Elsa

3. **A:** Juan doesn't have to work today.

   B: _____
   I

4. **A:** Room 101 needs towels.

   B: _____
   Room 102

5. **A:** I don't like to vacuum.

   B: _____
   I

2. Agreeing with <u>too</u> and <u>either</u>: present continuous and <u>be</u>

Present continuous: affirmative			
You	**are**	working.	I **am too**.
We	**are**		They **are too**.
He	**is**		She **is too**.

Negative			
You	**are**	not working.	I**'m not either**.
We	**are**		They**'re not either**.
He	**is**		She**'s not either**.

<u>Be</u>: affirmative			
You	**are**	ready.	I **am too**.
We	**are**		They **are too**.
He	**is**		She **is too**.

<u>Be</u>: negative			
You	**aren't**	ready.	I**'m not either**.
We	**aren't**		They**'re not either**.
He	**isn't**		She**'s not either**.

B. Complete the conversations. Use <u>too</u> or <u>either</u>.

1. **A:** Room 210 is clean. **B:** *Room 211 is too* .
   Room 211

2. **A:** I'm not working today. **B:** _____ .
   I

3. **A:** We're using the new furniture polish. **B:** _____ .
   They

4. **A:** She isn't wearing gloves. **B:** _____ .
   He

5. **A:** I'm in a hurry. **B:** _____ .
   I

6. **A:** We're not taking the 7:40 train. **B:** _____ .
   They

7. **A:** The 8:00 train is an express. **B:** _____ .
   The 8:20

C. Match the responses to the sentences. Write the letters.

_c_ **1.** She's not ready. **a.** I do too.

____ **2.** Yvonne has to work tomorrow. **b.** She is too.

____ **3.** They don't like cold weather. **c.** He isn't either.

____ **4.** He's always on time for work. **d.** I don't either.

3. <u>A</u>, <u>an</u>, and <u>the</u>

A / An	The
It's **an** <u>e</u>xpress train.	It's **the** 7:45 express to Rome.
Ed has **a** new car.	Ed's car is **the** one on **the** left.

Things to remember

1. Say <u>the</u> when your listener knows which specific thing you are talking about:
   the teacher's desk

2. Say <u>a</u> or <u>an</u> when you don't mean a specific thing. It is one of many:
   a desk in our classroom

3. Do not use <u>a</u> or <u>an</u> with non-count nouns:
   He bought glass cleaner.

4. Use <u>an</u> before vowel sounds:
   an apartment

D. Look at the pictures. Write **a**, **an**, or **the** on the line.

1. **A:** Could you get me ___*a*___ bucket?

   B: Which one?

   A: _____ large one.

2. **A:** I'm going to clean _____ mirror.

   B: You'll need _____ paper towel.

   A: Could you please get me _____ towel from _____ cart?

3. **A:** I'm looking for _____ apartment.

   B: I have _____ nice apartment for rent in this building.

   A: Which floor is it on?

   B: _____ ground floor.

---

4. The present continuous for the future

Subject	Present continuous	
I	**am going**	to a movie on Saturday.
We	**are leaving**	at 5:00 this afternoon.
He	**isn't working**	tomorrow.

E. Read Ana's note. Answer the questions. Use the present continuous.

DON'T FORGET!

Call the plumber this morning

2:30–take Pablo to the dentist

5:00–pick up Sophie

Tonight–go shopping with Luisa

1. When is Ana calling the plumber?

   She's calling the plumber this morning.

2. Where's Pablo going at 2:30?

   _____

3. What's Ana doing at 5:00?

   _____

4. What are Ana and Luisa doing tonight?

   _____

1. **If** in statements about the future with commands

If	Simple present tense	Command
If	the car **makes** a funny sound,	**take** it to a mechanic.
	the weather **is** bad,	**don't drive**.
	his fever **doesn't get** better tonight,	**call** the doctor.

Things to remember

1. Sentences with <u>if</u> have two clauses. You can change the order of the two clauses:
   If the weather is bad tomorrow, don't drive.
   Don't drive **if the weather is bad tomorrow**.
2. When the <u>if</u> clause is first in the sentence, use a comma. Do not use a comma when the <u>if</u> clause comes last.
3. Be careful! Use the simple present tense in the <u>if</u> clause. Don't use <u>will</u> in the <u>if</u> clause.
   If the weather is bad, don't drive.
   NOT ~~If the weather will be bad, don't drive.~~

A. Write the correct form of the verb.

1. Tell your employer if you _____*want*_____ a personal day next week.
   _{want}

2. Call me if you _____ busy this weekend.
   _{not / be}

3. Don't come to work if you _____ sick tomorrow.
   _{be}

4. If she _____ home soon, please call me.
   _{get}

5. If the weather _____ bad, stay home.
   _{be}

2. **If** in statements about the future with <u>will</u>

If	Simple present tense	Future with <u>will</u> / <u>won't</u>
If	it **rains** tomorrow,	we **won't go** to the park.
	my train **is** late,	I **will call** you.
	I **don't find** an apartment	I'**ll live** at home with my parents.

Things to remember

Be careful! Use the simple present tense in the <u>if</u> clause. Don't use <u>will</u> in the <u>if</u> clause.

If it rains tomorrow, we won't go to the park.
NOT ~~If it will rain tomorrow, we won't go to the park.~~

B. Choose the correct forms of the verbs. Write them on the lines.

1. If I _____*work*_____ the night shift, my wife _____*won't like*_____ it.
             work   not like

2. If it _____ nice tomorrow, we _____ lunch outside.
             be   have

3. If he _____ a promotion, he _____ more money.
             get   make

4. I _____ the job if they _____ it to me.
             accept   offer

5. You _____ well on the test if you _____ hard.
             do   study

3. <u>If</u> in questions about the future with present tense

Question word	<u>will</u>	Subject	Base form of the verb	<u>if</u> clause
	Will	she	call	**if** she wants to come?
	Will	they	tell us	**if** he gets the job?
What	**will**	you	do	**if** it rains?

C. Complete the questions with the correct form of the verbs.

1. _____*Will*_____ you _____*call*_____ me if you _____*need*_____ help?
                             call   need

2. What _____ we _____ if we _____ our new supervisor?
                             do   not like

3. _____ she _____ me if she _____ help?
                             tell   need

4. What _____ you _____ your boss if you _____ late?
                             tell   be

5. _____ Max _____ that camera if it _____ on sale?
                             buy   be

4. <u>Had better</u> in statements

Subject	<u>had better</u> / <u>had better not</u>	Base form of the verb	
I We You	**had better**	**go**	now.
They He She	**had better not**	**be**	late.

Things to remember
1. The contraction of <u>had better</u> = **'d better**
2. Be careful! Don't use <u>to</u> after <u>had better</u>.
We'd better go shopping.
NOT ~~We'd better to go shopping.~~

D. Complete the sentences with **'d better** or **'d better not** and words from the box.

park	smoke	~~stay~~	take	wear

1. She has a fever. She *'d better stay* _____ home.
2. It could rain. You _____ an umbrella.
3. You _____ there. That's the boss's parking spot.
4. It's cold outside. We _____ jackets.
5. You _____ in the building. It's against the law.

5. Would rather in statements

Subject	would rather / would rather not	Base form of the verb	
I We You	**would rather**	**go**	out.
They He She	**would rather not**	**stay**	at home.

Things to remember
1. The contraction of would rather = **'d rather**
2. Be careful! Don't use to after would rather.
She'd rather eat at home. NOT She'd rather to eat at home.

E. Look at the pictures. Complete the conversations. Use **'d rather**.

1. **A:** Does Marta want to be a bus driver?

   B: *No, she'd rather be a housekeeper.* _____

2. **A:** Does Alejandro want to play soccer?

   B: _____.

3. **A:** Would you like to get money inside the bank?

   B: _____.

4. **A:** Does Cindy like to take the train to work?

   B: _____.

5. **A:** Would Mr. Moon like to have a soda?

   B: _____.

<u>Would</u>	Subject	<u>rather</u>	Base form of the verb		<u>or</u>	Base form of the verb		Answers
Would	you	**rather**	**cook**		**or**	**wash**	dishes?	I'd rather cook.
	they		**eat**	here		**go**	out?	Go out.
	she		**take**	a bus			a train?	A train.

F. Complete the conversations. Write questions with <u>would rather</u>. Use <u>'d rather</u> in the answers.

1. **A:** <u>*Would your children rather eat chicken or fish?*</u>
                             your children / eat chicken or fish

   B: <u>*They'd rather*</u> eat chicken.

2. **A:** _____?
                your husband / work the day shift or the night shift

   B: I think _____ work days.

3. **A:** _____?
                you / make the beds or vacuum the carpet

   B: _____ not make the beds because my back hurts. So
   _____ vacuum, thanks.

4. **A:** _____?
                your co-workers / get more money or better benefits

   B: I'm not sure. I think _____ have better benefits.

5. **A:** _____?
                Pierre / live with his parents or his in-laws

   B: _____ not live with his in-laws. They don't get along.

U N I T   8

1. <u>Might</u>

Subject	<u>Might</u>	Base form of the verb
I We You They He She It	**might**	**fall**.
	might not	**work**.

Things to remember

1. Use the base form of the verb after <u>might</u> and <u>might not</u>.

2. Be careful! Don't use <u>to</u> after <u>might</u>.

She might take a personal day. NOT ~~She might to take a personal day.~~

A. Look at the pictures. Then complete the warnings. Use **might**.

1. Don't touch that! It's hot. You _____*might get burned*_____.
   get burned

2. Be careful. You _____.
   slip

3. Don't eat those. You _____.
   get sick

4. Don't run in the street! Drivers _____ you.
   not see

2. Responding with <u>I will</u> and <u>I won't</u> to express willingness

Command / warning		Response
Remember to	turn off the lights.	**I will.**
Don't forget to		**I won't.**

B. Complete each conversation with <u>I will</u> or <u>I won't</u>.

1. **A:** Don't forget to take your medicine twice a day.

   B: Don't worry. _*I won't*_____.

2. **A:** Jaywalking is dangerous. Cross the street at the light.

   B: OK. _____.

3. **A:** Remember to replace the batteries in the smoke detectors.

   B: _____.

4. **A:** You could get a shock, so don't touch that!

   B: Don't worry. _____.

5. **A:** If there is a fire, leave the building and call 911.

   B: All right, _____.

6. **A:** Please don't forget to test the fire extinguishers.

   B: _____.

1. Comparisons with adjectives: superlatives

- To form the superlative of short (usually, one-syllable*) adjectives, add –est to the adjective. Here are some spelling rules:
  1. For most adjectives, add –est.
     cheap → the cheap**est**   small → the small**est**
  2. For adjectives ending in <u>e</u>, add –st only.
     nice → the nice**st**   large → the large**st**
  3. For adjectives ending in <u>y</u>, change <u>y</u> to <u>i</u> and add –est.
     busy → the bus**iest**   early → the earl**iest**
  4. For adjectives ending in a consonant, vowel, consonant, double the final consonant and add –est.
     hot → the hot**test**   thin → the thin**nest**
- To form the comparative of most adjectives with two or more syllables, add <u>the most</u> before the adjective.
     the most expensive   **the most** interesting
- A few adjectives are irregular.
     good → the best   bad → the worst

*A syllable is a word or part of a word with one vowel sound: <u>cheap</u> has one syllable; <u>busy</u> has two syllables.

A. **Complete each sentence with the superlative form of the adjective.**

1. The tellers at First Bank are nicer than the ones at National Bank, but the ones at
   Key Credit Bank are _____*the nicest*_____ of all.
                                        nice

2. I don't go to the bank on Main Street. It always has _____
                                                                              long
   lines.

3. What are _____ questions to ask a bank officer?
                     important

4. I don't like credit cards. Cash is _____ thing for me.
                                              good

5. Where can I buy _____ gas in town?
                           cheap

6. Don't take your car there. They have _____ mechanics in
                                                  bad
   the city.

7. Many accidents happen in bathrooms. The bathroom is _____
                                                                 dangerous
   room in the house.

8. Which is _____ month of the summer?
                   hot

B. Look at the pictures. Complete the statements.

1. Western Bank is larger than Nutley
   Savings Bank, but First City Bank is
   _____ of the three banks.
   Nutley Savings Bank is _____
   of the three banks.

2. Julie is older than Olivia, but Lisa
   is _____ of the three
   sisters. Olivia is _____.

Lisa   Julie   Olivia

2. Questions of degree with How

How	Adjective / adverb		Answers
How	**old**	is Florence Savings Bank?	About 150 years.
	high	is the interest rate on your credit card?	I think it's 18%.
	good	is that hospital?	It's the best in the city.
	soon	can you be here?	In two hours.

C. Complete the conversations. Use **How** and a word from the box.

expensive	far	~~high~~	important	old

1. **A:** _How high_____ is the interest rate on a 6-month CD?
   B: I'm not sure. I think it used to be 3%.

2. **A:** _____ is the check-cashing office from here?
   B: You can walk there in three minutes.

3. **A:** _____ do you have to be to open a checking account?
   B: Eighteen, I think.

4. **A:** _____ is the restaurant?
   B: It's pretty expensive. It's the nicest restaurant in town, so it's not cheap!

5. **A:** _____ is a Personal Identification Number?
   B: Very important! You have to have a PIN to use the ATM.

UNIT 10

1. The present perfect: statements

Subject	have / has	Past participle	Subject	have / has	not	Past participle
I We You They	have	talked.	I We You They	have	not	talked.
He She It	has		He She It	has		

Things to remember

1. You can use these contractions in affirmative statements:

I + have = **I've**
we + have = **we've**
you + have = **you've**
they + have = **they've**

he + has = **he's**
she + has = **she's**
it + has = **it's**

2. You can use these contractions in negative statements:

has + not = **hasn't**
have + not = **haven't**

A. **Complete the sentences. Use the present perfect form of each verb.**

1. Mr. Young _____*has signed up*_____ for a medical plan, but he
   <u>sign up</u>

   _____ a doctor yet.
   <u>not choose</u>

2. I _____ to Louise in Benefits, but I _____ to my
   <u>speak</u>   <u>not talk</u>

   wife about a medical plan yet.

3. Mark and Rosa _____ the insurance information to read at
   <u>take</u>

   home. They _____ the information yet, but they will tonight.
   <u>not read</u>

4. Nilda _____ at Edison Lighting for six years. She
   <u>work</u>

   _____ a manager all that time. She got the job as a manager
   <u>not be</u>

   only two years ago.

Unit 10   **GB-27**

2. The present perfect with <u>already</u> and <u>yet</u>

Affirmative				Negative	
I **have**	already	**chosen** a medical plan.		I **haven't chosen** a plan	yet.
He **has**		**talked** to his doctor.		He **hasn't talked** to his doctor	

B. Complete the sentences. Use <u>already</u> or <u>yet</u>.

1. I have paid my gas bill, but I haven't paid my electric bill _____*yet*_____.

2. We have _____ taken all our vacation days this year.

3. Brad hasn't signed up for a medical plan _____.

4. I have _____ given you my co-payment.

5. I have _____ filled out a claim form.

6. I haven't gotten my reimbursement _____.

3. The present perfect with <u>since</u> and <u>for</u>

	since / for	
I have worked here	since	last year.
		1998.
	for	two years.
		10 months.

Things to remember
1. Use <u>since</u> followed by a specific point in time:
We have been busy **since 9:00**.
2. Use <u>for</u> followed by a length of time:
We have been busy **for two hours**.

C. Complete the sentences with the present perfect. Use <u>for</u> and <u>since</u>.

1. Joe ____*has been*____ unemployed ____*since*____ January 15.
   be

2. Kyoko started work here six months ago, so I _____ her
   know
   _____ six months.

3. My husband _____ a sore throat _____ three days.
   have

4. I _____ sick _____ last winter.
   not get

5. They _____ for that company _____ 1999.
   work

6. Ms. Clark _____ a sick day _____ last year.
   not take

Have/ has	Subject	Past participle	
Have	I you we they	started	**yet**?
Has	he she it		

Short answers							
Yes,	you I we they	**have**.	No,	you I we they	**haven't**.		
	he she it	**has**.		he she it	**hasn't**.		

Question word	have/ has	Subject	Past participle			Answers
How long	**have**	you	**known**	the Loyolas?		Since last summer.
	has	he	**worked**	there?		For eight weeks.

D. **Complete the conversations. Use the present perfect tense.**

1. **A:** _Have you taken_ _____ all your vacation days?
      <u>you / take</u>

   B: No, _I haven't_____. I'm going to take two days next week.

2. **A:** _____ always _____ a painter?
            <u>Felix / be</u>

   B: No, _____. He was an electrician in the Dominican Republic.

3. **A:** _____ in that medical plan?
            <u>How long / you / be</u>

   B: For about a year.

4. **A:** _____ for a dental plan?
            <u>your wife / sign up</u>

   B: Yes, _____.

5. **A:** _____ Marie?
            <u>How long / you / know</u>

   B: Since last year. We met at work.

6. **A:** _____ unemployed?
            <u>How long / Tina / be</u>

   B: Since last winter.

5. Be supposed to: statements

Subject	be	supposed to	Base form of the verb
I	am	supposed to	
You	are		call.
He	was	not supposed to	
We	were		

Things to remember
1. You can use contractions of <u>be</u> with <u>supposed to</u>, for example, I'm, you're, she's, they're, isn't, aren't, wasn't, weren't.
2. Use the base form of the verb after <u>be supposed to</u> and <u>be (not) supposed to</u>.

E. Look at the pictures and read the questions. Write two answers. Use <u>be supposed to</u>.

Jack—Northwest Medical called. Please call them back, and don't forget your appointment on Wed.

1. What is Alan supposed to do?
   a. _He's supposed to call_ Northwest Medical.
   b. _He's not supposed to forget_ his appointment.

Mom, I need you to pick me up after school, remember? Please don't be late!

2. What is Sherry supposed to do?
   a. _____ her son after school.
   b. _____ late.

Notice To All Employees

You must choose a doctor from the list on page 12. Don't go to a doctor who's not on the list or the plan will not reimburse you.

3. What are you supposed to do?
   a. _____ a doctor from the list.
   b. _____ a doctor who's not on the list.

You'll have to return this. You were supposed to get bathroom cleanser, but this is glass cleanser.

4. What was Dan supposed to do?
   a. _____ bathroom cleanser.
   b. _____ glass cleaner.

6. Be supposed to: questions

Be	Subject	supposed to	Base form of the verb
Am	I		
Is	he	**supposed to**	**call**?
Were	you		

Short answers

	you	**are**.		you	**aren't**.
Yes,	he	**is**.	No,	he	**isn't**.
	we	**were**.		we	**weren't**.

Question word	be	Subject	supposed to	Base form of the verb
When	**am**	I		**sign up**?
What	**are**	we	**supposed to**	**do**?
What time	**was**	he		**leave**?

Answers

Before Friday.
You're supposed to choose a medical plan.
An hour ago.

F. **Complete the questions. Use be supposed to.**

1. **A:** <u>When am I supposed to pay</u> the co-payment?
    When / I / pay

   B: You pay it when you visit the doctor.

2. **A:** Mr. Wong isn't here. He's late.

   B: _____ here?
           When / he / be

   A: Fifteen minutes ago.

3. **A:** _____ an enrollment form?
           I / fill out

   B: Yes, you are. You can do it at the Benefits Office.

4. **A:** _____ our eyes checked?
           we / get

   B: Yes, we are. You'll have to make an appointment with an optician.

5. **A:** I signed up for a medical plan. Now _____?
                                                 what / I / do

   B: Choose a doctor. It has to be a doctor on the list.

   A: _____ the list?
           Where / I / get

   B: Ask Pat in Benefits.

7. Suggestions with <u>Why</u>

<u>Why</u>	<u>don't</u>	Subject	Base form of the verb		Responses
Why	don't	you	**call**	me later?	OK, I will.
		we	**ask**	the office manager?	Good idea. Let's do that.

G. Complete the conversations. Write suggestions with <u>Why don't you</u> or <u>Why don't we</u>. Use words from the box.

eat outside	fill them out now	~~go to the Benefits Office~~
see a dentist	see an optician	call her

1. **A:** We need enrollment forms.

    B: <u>Why don't we go to the Benefits Office?</u>

    A: OK.

2. **A:** I think I need glasses.

    B: _____?

    A: Yes, I think I should.

3. **A:** Let's go to lunch, OK?

    B: Sure. You know, it's a beautiful day. _____?

    A: Good idea.

4. **A:** My tooth hurts.

    B: _____?

    A: I don't know a good dentist.

    B: Dr. Funamoto is good. _____?

5. **A:** We need to fill out the claim forms.

    B: _____?

    A: Good idea.

GB-32   **Grammar Booster**